Lohfeld Consulting Group

Insights

Volume 3

Capture & Proposal

Insights & Tips

Edited by Beth Wingate

Lohfeld Consulting Group

Insights

Capture & Proposal
Insights & Tips

Edited by Beth Wingate

Printed in United States of America
ISBN: 978-0-9887554-8-2

Published by Lohfeld Consulting Group, Inc.
940 South River Landing Road
Edgewater, Maryland 21037

For more information, contact BWingate@LohfeldConsulting.com

Production, Design, and Copyediting: Alexandra Wingate

| Dedication

We dedicate this third Insights book to our families, whose daily support enables us to do what we love best, and to our colleagues, whose positive reviews of our books and continuing encouragement compelled us to share more insights and tips with our capture and proposal community.

| About the authors

Brenda Crist, Vice President, APMP Fellow

Brenda Crist serves as a senior capture and proposal manager and develops strategic solutions for clients. She focuses on helping clients work with their staff and partners to create winning, well-written proposal solutions. She offers hands-on experience from leading and conducting systems and network management projects for many civilian and military clients.

Brenda Crist has more than 25 years' experience providing capture, proposal, and program management support for companies serving the federal market. She supports companies by helping to qualify new business opportunities, conducting research, performing competitive analyses, providing capture support, managing proposals, and writing and reviewing proposals. Her areas of expertise include the civilian IT, health, and scientific markets. Brenda is an experienced trainer focusing on business development for project managers, proposal writing and management, and APMP Foundation Level Certification.

Brenda stays current with the latest procurements, their requirements, and industry best practices. She served as the 2010 President and formerly as 2009 Vice President and Professional Day Chairperson for the Association of Proposal Management Professionals (APMP), National Capital Area (NCA) Chapter. She has been an active member of APMP-NCA since 2003, serving as Professional Day Chair of Publicity, Speakers Program, and Chairperson for the 2006, 2007, and 2008 events, respectively.

Brenda was inducted as an APMP Fellow in June 2011 and also received the Steven S. Myers Award for 2011 APMP Chapter Chair of the Year. She holds an MPA, Public Administration from American University and is Information Technology Infrastructure Library (ITIL) certified.

Wendy Frieman, The Proposal Doctor, APMP Fellow

Wendy Frieman is a proposal and capture manager with 25+ years of experience leading teams to win government contracts. Formerly a Principal Consultant with Lohfeld Consulting Group, she has worked at large and small companies, including Oracle, SAIC, CSC, and Chenega. Her experience spans multiple domains and industries: science and technology, policy, telecom, national security and intelligence, systems integration, and software. She is an APMP Fellow and holds APMP Professional-level certification.

Maryann Lesnick, Managing Director

Maryann brings more than 25 years of experience in business development; proposal management, writing, and editing; capture management; project management; and quality management for both federal and commercial sectors. She holds APMP Practitioner-level certification (CP APMP) and is a Project Management Institute (PMI) certified Project Management Professional (PMP). She is also a Certified Scrum Master (CSM) and certified Microsoft Office Specialist (MOS).

Since 1979, Maryann has prepared hundreds of winning proposals for contracts and task orders, written and oral, ranging in value from $2M to $1.5B. Major customers include Federal Agencies (Department of Defense, Department of Homeland Security, Department of Justice, Small Business Administration, National Institutes of Health, Department of Labor, Environmental Protection Agency, and U.S. Postal Service), and state and local customers (Virginia, New York State, Georgia, New York City, and San Francisco).

Prior to joining Lohfeld Consulting Group, Maryann served as Vice President of Proposals for Base Technologies (later CA Technologies) where she supported the entire business development lifecycle and led all public sector services bids. She served as proposal manager, volume manager, editor, color team facilitator, capture manager, and writer. She established an ISO 9001:2008-compliant proposal development methodology. She also built and maintained a knowledge base for proposal artifacts, boilerplate, past performance/project summaries, and resumes.

Maryann has been active with APMP for the past 13 years, has served on the Board of Directors of the NCA chapter for the past 8 years, and served as the 2014–2015 APMP-NCA President. She currently serves as NCA Chapter Membership Chair and is on the Board of Directors for APMP International.

Bob Lohfeld, CEO & Founder, APMP Fellow

Bob Lohfeld has more than 30 years' experience winning contracts in the government market and is recognized consistently for leadership in business development, capture management, and winning proposals development.

He teaches Capture Management, and he writes the Capture Management column in *Washington Technology* magazine. Prior to forming Lohfeld Consulting Group, Bob served as Division President at Lockheed Martin, Vice President of Lockheed Martin Information Technology, Senior Vice President at OAO Corp., Systems Engineering Manager at Computer Sciences Corp. (CSC), and Program Manager at Fairchild Industries. He also taught at the graduate level at George Washington University School of Engineering Administration.

Bob has served on the Board of Directors for APMP and APMP-NCA and as Chairman of the American Council on Technology Industry Advisory Council (ACT/IAC), Vice Chairman of the Technology Council of Maryland (TCM), and Board Member of the Armed Forces Communications and Electronics Association (AFCEA), Government Electronics and Information Association (GEIA), and Juvenile Diabetes Research Foundation (JDRF Capital Region). He is a three-time winner of *Federal Computer Week's* Federal 100.

Lisa Pafe, Vice President, APMP Fellow

Lisa brings more than 25 years' experience in business development, capture and proposal management, process improvement, and training. She is an APMP Fellow and holds APMP Professional-level certification (CPP APMP Fellow). She is a PMI certified PMP. Lisa is also a trained Internal Auditor for ISO 9001:2008. She has managed hundreds of winning government proposals, writes and speaks extensively, and is a recognized thought leader in the proposal industry.

As Vice President of Corporate Development and Proposal Operations for Ace Info Solutions, Inc., Lisa was responsible for the company's full opportunity life cycle, including positioning to win through branding, marketing, BD, strategic teaming arrangements, and capture and proposal management activities. Previously, she was President of Vision Consulting, Inc.; Vice President of Business Development for GovConnect, Inc.; and Director of Marketing Services for MAXIMUS, Inc.

Lisa is the 2016 President of the APMP-NCA Chapter and previously served as Vice President and Speaker Series Chair.

Julia Quigley, Operations and Training Manager

Julia's operations support is backed by proposal management experience for federal contracts and a background in writing instruction. She has worked on a variety of Federal Health IT task orders and large proposals. With a Master's in Rhetoric and Composition, she has conducted proposal writing strategies and training to help technical subject matter experts understand how to respond clearly and compellingly to solicitation requirements.

Prior to joining Lohfeld Consulting Group, she worked at small and mid-sized federal contractors and at Texas State University. The federal contracting environments provided insight into the gamut of proposal activities—from capture, to bid development, to contracts—that allows her to better understand Lohfeld clients' needs. At Texas State University, she taught introductory writing and persuasive writing classes. She applies the lessons she taught as well as the lessons learned to all her writing and training projects. Julia presented at the 2016 APMP Bid & Proposal Con.

Beth Wingate, President, APMP Fellow

Beth Wingate has more than 25 years' proposal development, management, and corporate communications experience. She helps clients develop proposals, improve their proposal operations, and build their corporate communications programs. An excellent, experienced proposal manager, Beth specializes in managing responses to large government procurements as well as task order proposals.

Prior to joining our firm, she served as proposal center director for Lockheed Martin and before that for 12 years as proposal center director for Management Systems Designers, Inc. (MSD) (acquired by Lockheed Martin).

Beth was inducted as an APMP Fellow in June 2010. She is APMP's 2014 Past CEO, 2013 CEO, 2012 COO, 2010–2011 Director of Education, and 2008 and 2009 President of the APMP-NCA Chapter. She served as the Chapter's *Executive Summary* Newsletter Chairperson, publisher, and editor from 2005 to 2007. Beth received the Steven S. Myers Award for 2008 APMP Chapter Chair of the Year. She regularly presents at APMP International and Regional conferences. She has been an active APMP member since 1996.

Contents

Insights

Capture & Proposal Insights and Tips – Volume 3

Insights

Capture & Proposal Insights and Tips – Volume 3

Insights

Capture & Proposal Insights and Tips – Volume 3

Capture

Capture and proposal innovations: activate your listening campaign

Lisa Pafe

What do customers really want? As capture and proposal professionals, that question haunts us. We work very hard to understand customer hot buttons and craft our solution accordingly. However, too often, the proposal focuses too much on our solution and too little on articulating a value proposition that truly reflects the customers' desires.

As you strive to understand what is *behind the curtain,* take an honest look at your listening skills. We often schedule meetings with customers and spend most of the allotted time presenting our capabilities rather than listening to the customers' wants and needs. In reality, your capture plan should be 90% about listening and 10% about talking.

However, *listening*, as opposed to *hearing*, is a learned skill that requires active, conscious effort. So, how can you best embark on an innovative listening campaign?

The "customer" is really the "customers"

You may have noticed that I refer to the customer in the plural. Remember, a single customer does not exist. Each opportunity has many stakeholders: programmatic, technical, subject matter experts, acquisition, and executives. Your listening campaign must include all of them.

If possible, identify and engage with the full gamut of leaders, influencers, followers, and decision-makers.

Listen to employees too

Engagement need not be directly with the customers. Current and former employees of the customer organization, the incumbent contractor, if there is one, and teaming partners will often be quite honest with you regarding problem areas as well as potential successful strategies. Research employees on LinkedIn and reach out. Make sure to use personal emails or LinkedIn messages after hours to avoid disruption to the workday.

Ask specific questions

Instead of asking the customers what you can do to help them, suggest solutions and listen to their reaction. Ask very specific questions that require them to answer with examples. For instance, ask customers about:

- Acquisition strategy requirements, preferred vehicles, and key evaluation factor preferences for this procurement.
- Technology requirements and preferences.
- Negotiable and non-negotiable requirements.
- Performance level and customer satisfaction expectations.
- Mission and program objectives, both qualitative and quantitative.
- Transition timing.
- Budget, change, and risk tolerances.
- Other drivers such as Executive Orders, Congressional mandates, and the like.

Moving from general to specific questions generates a higher level of engagement as well as the more thoughtful and detailed responses that will provide the insights you are seeking. For better results, invest the time to improve your questioning techniques (https://goo.gl/bywdvL).

Shape the opportunity

Without shaping, you are at a real disadvantage. Shaping is more about listening to stakeholders and then using that information to suggest scope, evaluation factors, procurement vehicles, technologies, and the like that will work well. Propose ideas based on evidence and listen to the reaction. Come back with new ideas and listen some more.

Once the RFP is released, analyze the solicitation to ensure it reflects the shaping you think you accomplished. If it doesn't, seriously re-evaluate your bid decision and/or adapt your solution accordingly.

Identify unanswered questions

Knowledge gaps may require that you identify additional stakeholders with whom to engage and/or identify new or better questions. Make sure all gaps are covered prior to RFP release and that you have fully listened, shaped, and tested your value proposition with customers.

Avoid jargon and acronyms

Often we fall into the habit of using idioms, acronyms, and complex terminology. Customers may not fully understand what you are saying. Try speaking in plain English for greater clarity of intent.

Repeat, repeat, repeat

When customers talk, repeat what you think they said to gain confirmation. When you talk, ask each meeting participant to offer their perspective on and/or summary of what you just said. By making everyone re-frame their understanding, you will gain greater precision. Poor listening is costly because it results in incorrect assumptions surrounding win strategy, misunderstanding of the desired value proposition, and errors that waste Bid and Proposal (B&P) money. Understanding what the customer really wants begins and ends with your listening skill innovations.

Discriminating your offer: 5 steps to competitive edge

Lisa Pafe

As we look back on last year and ahead to the challenges of the next, it is clear you must find ways to discriminate your bid from the competition. Discriminating your offer is especially difficult for service providers (versus product providers) as the playing field is fairly level and more bidders are competing for less work. Market competition is a battleground, and your goal should be to win the war…or at least the *must-win* battles that comprise your target revenues.

In my experience, five steps are key to gaining competitive edge and discriminating yourself from the competition.

1. **Understand your industry.** First things first! In order to discriminate your bid, you must know who your competitors are. Amazingly, many companies have cut their competitive intelligence capabilities due to

budget constraints. Reserve enough B&P dollars to at least research your industry and lines of business using subscription services, key word searches, and social media. Ask your customers their opinions as to who the best and worst companies are.

2. **Analyze the competitors.** Studying the competition allows you to find weaknesses. Perform ethical stalking. Subscribe to their newsletters. Check out their employees on LinkedIn. Search social media. Buy a product and note the logistics of the sales process. Network and speak to executives as many of these leaders will brag about accomplishments. Take note and begin to brainstorm ideas for setting your bid apart.

3. **Put your findings to good use.** Often, we gather information but fail to act on it. Once you understand the *Who* and the *What*, you can begin to identify the *How*. The *How* involves carefully perfecting your proposed strengths. By strengths, I mean ways you can exceed customer requirements without increasing costs. Strengths are not easy to identify in the services industry, but

examples include creating the best customer service experience for increased user satisfaction; value-adds such as access to industry experts, training, research labs, and/or white papers; and/or increased efficiency and effectiveness through better Key Performance Indicators (KPIs), Service Level Agreements (SLAs), and preventive action.

4. **Fly under the radar.** Meet with the customer to express your strengths, but avoid showcasing these strengths in public forums. After all, your competitors are performing the same ethical stalking as you are. If your company is over-exposed, then competitors will respond by ghosting your company in order to gain market share. Create quiet opportunities with the advance work you do during the capture phase with a focus on shaping upcoming bids in your favor and winning sole source work wherever possible.

5. **Continually improve.** With increased competition, the only way to maintain your lead is to stay one step ahead of the competition. Continual improvement

requires investment in understanding and growing capabilities to future advances in both products and services. It also requires that you keep existing customers more than satisfied by looking for ways to improve their experience through feedback loops and proactive improvement to retain their loyalty.

Proposal Production

Avoid the Red Team II Monster by implementing efficiencies

Brenda Crist

There is nothing more I dread than a Red Team II or even a Red Team III. It means the entire bid and proposal team didn't produce a compliant, strong, and compelling proposal. In addition to inviting the concern of executive leadership and dragging down the morale of the entire bid team, Red Team IIs or IIIs also result in long days and weekends full of work.

I try to avoid them at any cost. My best defense is a good offense. If I am lucky, I will join the effort before the solicitation is released so I can work with the capture manager or team to develop an information-collection plan, frame the solution, validate it with the customer, and optimize it. This is not often the case, because as a consultant, I usually arrive after the RFP is released.

In my experience, what the team does the first week after a solicitation is released can have a tremendous impact on whether we end up working long days and weekends. Here are five timesaving processes I implement in addition to a good Kick-off Meeting to gain efficiencies:

1. Conduct a compliance review.
2. Conduct a solution review.
3. Conduct a price review.
4. Communicate the solution to the team.
5. Create a production plan.

Conduct a compliance review

As soon as the RFP is released, I prepare a compliance matrix that maps solicitation requirements to the proposal response. The task can often be more of an art than a science because I often find the instructions, evaluation criteria, and requirements are not clear, are conflicting, or are two–three times larger than the page limitations. I recommend having the capture manager/bid team lead and a few members of the bid team review the compliance matrix to verify it will result in a compliant response. If the team has questions, they should immediately submit written questions to the Contracting Officer to resolve them.

Conduct a solution review

The solicitation release invariably causes some changes to the pre-solicitation solution. I recommend conducting technical, management, and past performance reviews to determine how solution gaps can be filled, how weaknesses can be mitigated, and how strengths can be optimized and further substantiated by solid, quantitative proof points. The bid team should quickly compare their updated solution to the customer's evaluation criteria and verify that it can still be highly ranked, and if not, determine what needs to be done to raise the score. The solution should be frozen as soon as possible—barring any unforeseen changes caused by final pricing or amendments.

Conduct a price review

Once the solution is frozen, I recommend the pricing team verify they have all the information to generate the pricing volume and that they immediately alert the capture manager and technical volume lead if they must change or tweak the solution to fit their price-to-win model.

The pricing team should also communicate pricing requirements to the subcontractors, immediately determine if they are showstoppers, and communicate their findings to the capture and proposal managers.

Communicate the solution to the team

By the end of the first week, the solution architect, business lead, and past performance lead should be able to communicate the solution strengths to all the proposal writers and company executives. All writers should understand how to communicate the company's strengths, mitigate its weaknesses, ghost the competition, and present a clear and compelling approach from the customer's point of view.

Create a production plan

The very last thing I do during Week 1 is to create a production plan that describes how we will edit/review, produce, and ship the proposal in compliance with the customer's requirements. I produce primary and contingency plans for production and ensure we leave at least 10% of the proposal schedule for production.

In summary, producing a compliant proposal outline, generating a *strengths-rich* solution with a correlated price, and effectively communicating the solution to the proposal writers as soon as possible after the solicitation release will help banish the Red Team II Monster. Creating a sound production plan well in advance of the proposal due date will ensure your proposal is delivered on time.

Reprinted with permission from the APMP-NCA Executive Summary.

An agile retrospective

Maryann Lesnick

Looking back at the past and into the future makes me think of the proposal postmortem. Performing a critical lessons learned review of what worked well and what can be improved is an important best practice in the lifecycle of a proposal. Do we always have at least one? How much attention do we give it before rushing off to the next proposal?

Agile approaches like Scrum and Kanban employ a similar best practice called the Agile Retrospective. Its purpose is the same as a proposal postmortem—to capture lessons learned and improve processes and outcomes on future sprints (or proposal efforts). What can we learn from our counterparts in the software engineering field? What new perspectives can we adopt from the agile principles? After all, we are all developing a product—theirs is software, and ours is the proposal.

Retrospective (from Latin *retrospectare,* "look back") refers to looking back at past events. In the context of both proposal and IT projects, it is a meeting held by a team at the end of a project/process/iteration/cycle/sprint to discuss what was successful, what can be improved, and how to incorporate the successes and improvements in future projects. This discussion also gives the team members a chance to inspect and adapt their behavior and reaction to the current state of the process and helps them devise ways to improve coordination and collaboration.

Retrospectives are widely considered one of the most important and indispensable Agile techniques. Inspection and adaptation are all about continuous improvement, and without continuous improvement, there is no true sense to the term *agility*.

Agile Retrospective: The five-phase structure

Agile Retrospectives are not just a quick *round robin* over coffee and donuts. A good Retrospective has structure and requires preparation. In the book *Agile Retrospectives: Making Good Teams Great,* Esther Derby and Diana Larsen identify five steps the facilitator should follow when conducting a Retrospective.

1. **Set the stage.** Lay the groundwork for the session by reviewing the goals and agenda. Create an environment for participation by

checking in and establishing working agreements.

2. **Gather data.** Review objective and subjective information to create a shared picture. Capture each person's perspective. Seeing the iteration from many points of view provides greater insight.

3. **Generate insights.** Step back and look at the picture the team has created. Use activities that help people think together to delve beneath the surface.

4. **Decide what to do.** Prioritize the team's insights and choose a few improvements or experiments that will make a difference on future efforts.

5. **Close the Retrospective.** Summarize how the team will follow up on plans and commitments. Thank team members for their hard work. Conduct a Retrospective on the Retrospective. The Scrum Master (proposal manager) usually facilitates the Retrospective, and part of his/her job is to make sure that all participants know they can speak their mind. *Working agreements*

include recognizing that all viewpoints have merit.

Data gathering involves examining:

1. **What worked well?** List the processes, interactions, and events that the team found helpful and would like to continue.

2. **What didn't work well?** List the delays, impediments, and broken processes that the team would like to either improve or discontinue.

3. **What actions can we take to improve our process going forward?** List the improvements and actions that can be carried forward into future sprints based on the lessons learned in the Retrospective.

One technique Agile teams use to collect ideas at a Retrospective is to use Post-its or a white board to capture all ideas on the wall. The team puts forth ideas/suggestions for improvement and collectively decides which to carry forward for future projects.

There are other techniques, games, and simulations that Agile teams use to promote a creative and comfortable platform for team members to express themselves freely. These games make the Retrospective meeting more productive, interactive, and fun.

As a rule of thumb, a Retrospective for a 30-day sprint lasts about 4 hours. How much time do we as proposal managers take for a Retrospective? Another Agile rule of thumb is to make sure at least one actionable item comes out of each Retrospective session. Do we always have a Retrospective, or post-mortem at the end of a proposal effort? Perhaps we are not putting enough focus on this activity?

Conclusions

In summary, consider approaching the Proposal Postmortem with renewed focus:

- Always have one.
- Make it a priority.
- Make sure at least one actionable component comes out of each meeting.

Agile practices place a high degree of importance on the Retrospective. Retrospectives are planned, executed, and revisited with a follow-up at the same level as Agile code inspections (or our color team reviews). Perhaps we should treat the proposal postmortem like another color team?

Insights

Capture & Proposal Insights and Tips – Volume 3

Let's treat the proposal postmortem like another color review, giving it the planning, execution, and follow-up it deserves!

Learning about brain syncing with SMEs from Instructional Design

Three-part process for brain syncing with SMEs

Julia Quigley

Interviewing SMEs for course design has several parallels with interviewing SMEs for proposal content. Course designers and proposal writers are usually content neutral, and both designers and writers need enough expert information about a topic to clearly describe how a task will be/should be performed. Further, designers and writers often have limited access to experts, resulting in condensed and intense interactions. Given these similarities, it may come as no surprise that a course designer's process and artifacts for interviewing SMEs align with proposal writing best practices.

Information designer Connie Malamed's three-part process for brain syncing with SMEs (https://goo.gl/iEmB0) is a solid approach for anyone interviewing a SME for a proposal. Malamed's three phases and key takeaways from each phase include:

Phase 1: Prep work

- Read ahead on background materials; gain a general understanding of the subject matter.
- Write out specific questions in advance and create a plan for the interview.
- Provide the SME with a time estimate and your questions in advance, if possible.

Phase 2: The interview

- Be appreciative! Gratitude goes a long way.
- Record the interview, if possible.
- Stop occasionally and paraphrase concepts back to your SME to verify you're understanding the information correctly.

Phase 3: Follow-up

- Review and organize your notes immediately, while everything is fresh in your brain.
- Listen to the recording to include or correct details you missed in your notes.

- Note any gaps in knowledge and contact the SME to provide additional information.

This three-step process provides a solid structure with lessons-learned instilled. Winging it or not giving your SME time to prepare can tank what would have been a fruitful meeting, so having a plan and prepping your SME will maximize what you get out of the meeting. Even if you're a skilled interviewer, remember that your SME may not be familiar with the process, so explain these phases as soon as you can.

To facilitate note-taking and structuring the interview, Malamed provides a content collection form by Abigail Wheeler (https://goo.gl/PiaotH), a learning and development project manager at a firm that consults to government agencies and nonprofit organizations. While her collection form is geared toward learning objectives, many of questions are similar to those a proposal writer might ask. I reworded the questions but kept the same overall structure to develop this guide for interviewing a SME for a proposal.

Subject Matter Expert Content Collection Form

Proposal section	Insert the title of proposal section
PWS requirements	List the PWS requirements for this section, grouping like requirements together if they aren't already logically organized within the solicitation
Lesson description	Insert lesson description from approved design plan
Major Task 1	Insert the first major task (it's possible several PWS "shall statements" fall under a single task)
Key information	What activities will our workers perform in order to achieve this major task? Please provide two to five paragraphs, up to 700 words.
Key skills & technologies	What skill and programs will the worker(s) use to perform the major task and any sub-tasks? Please provide one to two paragraphs.
Image suggestions	What images, metaphors, models, or diagrams are useful for understanding the activities and processes?
Benefits	• Explain the benefits to doing the work as described above, compared with other possible approaches. • Clearly describe at least X number of benefits and how they're derived from the approach described above.
Scenarios/case examples	• Describe one or more appropriate scenarios related to this learning objective. • If we run into a certain risk or scenario, how will we address the scenario? • Based on our knowledge of the current environment, are there are any optimizations to current processes we'll be making?
Resources	What resources or references do you suggest to learners to explore information and skills related to this objective further?
Major Task 2	Insert the second major task (it's possible several PWS "shall statements" fall under a single task)
Key information	What activities will our workers perform in order to achieve this major task? Please provide two to five paragraphs, up to 700 words.
Key skills & technologies	What skill and programs will the worker(s) use to perform the major task and any sub-tasks? Please provide one to two paragraphs.
Image suggestions	What images, metaphors, models, or diagrams are useful for understanding the activities and processes?
Benefits	• Explain the benefits to doing the work as described above, compared with other possible approaches. • Clearly describe at least X number of benefits and how they're derived from the approach described above.
Scenarios/case examples	• Describe one or more appropriate scenarios related to this learning objective. • If we run into a certain risk or scenario, how will we address the scenario? • Based on our knowledge of the current environment, are there are any optimizations to current processes we'll be making?
Resources	What resources or references do you suggest to learners to explore information and skills related to this objective further?

Major Task 3	Insert the first major task (it's possible several PWS "shall statements" fall under a single task)
Key information	What activities will our workers perform in order to achieve this major task? Please provide two to five paragraphs, up to 700 words.
Key skills & technologies	What skill and programs will the worker(s) use to perform the major task and any sub-tasks? Please provide one to two paragraphs.
Image suggestions	What images, metaphors, models, or diagrams are useful for understanding the activities and processes?
Benefits	• Explain the benefits to doing the work as described above, compared with other possible approaches. • Clearly describe at least X number of benefits and how they're derived from the approach described above.
Scenarios/case examples	• Describe one or more appropriate scenarios related to this learning objective. • If we run into a certain risk or scenario, how will we address the scenario? • Based on our knowledge of the current environment, are there are any optimizations to current processes we'll be making?
Resources	What resources or references do you suggest to learners to explore information and skills related to this objective further?

This form doesn't replace good prep work and planning, but it provides a structure to organize the conversation and resulting information.

What tips and strategies do you use when interviewing SMEs? Do you use forms or fly by the seat of your pants?

How to select the right consultant for you

If locating and vetting consultant support is overwhelming your team, consider these tips for finding the best match for your needs

Julia Quigley

With decreased federal budgets, there's more competition for contractors than ever before. Whether you're trying to get an edge on a *must win* opportunity, increase your capacity to respond to proposals, or just keep your staff from burning out, you may turn to proposal consultants.

Finding the right consultant can be a challenge. You need someone who's effective and who's a good fit for your mission-critical objective. How do you find the right one?

What to look for

Any consultant you consider should have basic qualifications, such as the following:

- **Reputation:** Known for quality support with a legacy of winning and added value.
- **Experience:** Adequate years of specific, current proposal experience (at least 15–20 years for senior-level support).
- **Leadership:** Proven leadership within our industry or professional organizations.
- **Autonomy:** Self-sufficiency; a proven ability to work independently.
- **Expertise:** Specialization with a multi-faceted skill set; familiar with the business development lifecycle.
- **Knowledge:** Ability to implement best practices and enhance existing process, while maintaining flexibility with existing processes.
- **Familiarity:** Relevant domain experience, specific to industry, agency, and/or subject matter.
- **Skilled:** Relevant training and certifications.
- **Equipped:** Solid experience using industry-standard tools (Microsoft Office,

SharePoint, other content management systems, etc.).

Reputation is one of the most important, but often overlooked, qualifications. Proven ability to provide quality service and added value is a better predictor of success than any other qualification. Don't invest thousands of dollars on an unknown entity. As you distinguish between possibilities, consider whether the resource will simply help with your immediate needs or if the consultant will provide added value by helping you improve your processes and mentor current staff members.

What to avoid

Avoid the lowest price options. Quality consulting that yields winning bids costs a premium price. Federal contractors know this and are willing to spend money to make money. If you come across a consultant with low prices, carefully investigate why that person isn't able to charge the *going rate*.

Where to find consultants

Once you're equipped with vetting criteria and you know what to look for, there are three primary resources for finding consultants: job sites listing independent consultants, resume shops, and consulting firms.

Independent consultants. Recent downsizing in the federal market flooded the beltway with independent consultants. Some are outstanding and some are not. It's often hard to tell the difference until you see their work products. With careful vetting, you can find an expert, but if you're dissatisfied there's no quality guarantee backing you up.

Resume shops. Resume shops maintain a database of resumes and present options based on how much you're willing to pay and how many years of experience you're looking for. This process will save you a tremendous amount of time compared to finding independent consultants on your own, but there's still limited accountability for performance.

Consulting firms. A consulting firm is the best place to locate a proposal consultant because their consultants are pre-vetted, and you're dealing with a company invested in protecting their reputation by providing you with outstanding support.

A quality consulting firm will provide you with consultants across the country who are already vetted, insured, cleared, and who have signed an ethics policy. Does the firm you're talking with employ industry experts to vet their consultants?

In addition to finding talented experts, a consulting firm manages their consultant's performance for optimum customer satisfaction. Does the firm you're talking with conduct regular customer satisfaction surveys?

You're likely to get the best fit if you locate a consultant through a consulting firm. The firm can match you with the right consultant because they know their consultants' personalities, abilities, and track records. Common processes and perspectives in the firm mean continuity of support over time with different consultants on different projects.

Making a selection

As you look for a consultant to support your needs, ask yourself how much time you're willing to invest in finding and vetting a resource yourself. Are you comfortable assuming the risk and responsibility of procuring someone from an online job board or a resume shop? You'll save time and get better results by trusting a proven consulting firm to match you with an expert consultant that meets your needs.

Insights

Capture & Proposal Insights and Tips – Volume 3

Writing to Win

Improving the quality of proposal content with a writing model – Part 1

Spend time training your proposal writers

Julia Quigley

Proposal managers are frequently faced with the challenge of proposal resources who can't write well. We are often assigned technical resources with a reputation for poor writing and new resources whose lack of familiarity with proposals is reflected in their content submissions. This creates a lot of extra work for proposal managers to *fix* sections, and the rough content disrupts color reviews. Inevitably, reviewers either can't resist the urge to redline the document, or they're so frustrated trying to understand convoluted language that they mentally check out. Neither of these options leads to effective reviews that validate the content or improve the proposal.

When faced with the challenge of unskilled writers, I've seen proposal managers take one or more of the following actions:

- Interview the resource and write the section for themselves.
- Pair the writer up with a more experienced writer (often assigned to another section).
- Give the writer boilerplate or prior proposal text to adapt.

One option I don't see proposal managers pursuing is training and education. Education is the best option for return on investment, reducing the burden for other proposal team members, and improving your color review process. After your initial investment to increase the skill level of a proposal resource, you see the benefits on every additional proposal that resource works on. Other team members won't be burdened by picking up this unskilled writer's work, and you won't have to take time interviewing and writing for your resource. Finally, color reviews will be more effective because reviewers won't be distracted by poor writing. Once your resources provide the reviewers with clean, clear text, the reviewers can focus on reviewing the content rather than the form.

Perhaps proposal managers don't pursue training because they don't think it's a feasible option. Training usually requires outside resources and buy-in from the trainee or the trainer. Further, there's often the idea that if someone didn't learn how to write well in high school or college, they won't learn it for proposals.

In contrast with these perspectives, a proposal manager can provide minimal just-in-time training to achieve remarkably improved proposal text. I have put in as little as 2 hours of training—in the form of a lunch-and-learn combined with some individual feedback—and seen considerable improvements in proposal content's organization, clarity, and content from inexperienced and technical writers alike. This approach required no outside resources or extra funding, and the benefits were realized on several proposals.

Now that you're (hopefully) convinced that training your reticent writers is beneficial and feasible, tune back in for the next parts of this series where I'll cover what to teach your writers and how you can institutionalize these methods in your proposal teams.

Improving the quality of proposal content with the APB writing model – Part 2

The APB method simplifies writing tasks and makes it easy for the government to evaluate your text

Julia Quigley

In the last post of the APB writing model series, I argued that training your proposal team to follow a standard writing model is the best approach for improving proposal content. In this post, I'll introduce you to the APB writing model you should implement and describe the benefits this writing model achieves. After reading this post, you'll be ready to transform your bids.

The APB model stands for *approach, process,* and *benefits*. I liken the APB model to a police officer's *All Points Bulletin*. A cop's APB makes what they're looking for abundantly clear so other officers won't miss it. In the same way, your writing needs to make your strengths abundantly clear to evaluators so they won't miss them. The APB structure gives the evaluators all the detail in an easy-to-read format so they can find and record those strengths and rate your proposal as *outstanding*. In addition to making it easy on evaluators, this model provides structure for inexperienced writers and helps reign in writers who know a lot of information but can't write well.

In practice, APB is a model for developing paragraphs of text within your response:

- **Approach.** The Approach is the first one to three sentences at the beginning of your paragraph that briefly summarizes your approach and benefits. It's your elevator speech. These sentences overview what you will do for the client and what benefits your clients will receive.
- **Process.** The process section is the meat of your paragraph, containing all the details and graphics the government needs to evaluate your solution. Include the steps, tools, and methodologies you will use to accomplish that approach. This section

includes all the features you identified in pre-proposal planning.

- **Benefits.** The benefits explanation forms a logical end cap. While you previewed your benefits in the approach summary section, conclude your paragraph with one to three sentences that fully explain how the process yields those benefits. You can include proof points and substantiation in the benefits section to conclude your paragraph, or you may include them immediately after you introduce a feature in the process section.

While the model is based on a paragraph structure, you may scale this up or down to suit your needs. If your requirements and page count call for more detail, make the A, P, and B each their own paragraph. If you go this route, you may even break the process section up into multiple paragraphs with strong transition sentences. On the other hand, if you're responding to very simple requirements, you may want to shrink APB into just a few sentences in a very small paragraph.

However you scale the model, packaging your text into APB makes it easy for evaluators to find the content they're looking for. Evaluators don't read proposals, they score them. Putting key words and benefits at the beginning and end of paragraphs makes it easy for skimmers to identify the strengths of your proposal.

To exemplify the power of the APB model, consider this fictitious example. Let's say our client has put out a requirement for us to protect a wood deck for at least 5 years. I generally see two kinds of non-APB responses:

1. We will protect your wood deck for at least 5 years with industry-best tools and equipment.

2. Two of our senior carpenters will protect your wood deck for at least 5 years by applying two coats of Behr waterproof stain with a three-inch bristle brush.

The first is the bare minimum of written text. It parrots back the requirement without adding any value. The phrase "industry-best tools and equipment" is so vague it doesn't mean anything to evaluators. This kind of non-APB writing is asking the government to trust us that we can do what we say we will do for them.

The second option is better, but it lacks the compelling features of an APB structure. The second option adds value by explaining how we're going to fulfill the requirements, but it makes the reader do all the work about what benefits they're going to see and what the strengths of our approach are. This is a problem because we need to do the work for our readers.

In contrast, the APB example below contains the same information, but packages it so that an evaluator can easily score the section.

> **A.** We will protect the deck for 10 years by applying two coats of waterproof stain with tools to deeply penetrate the wood.
>
> **P.** Two of our senior carpenters will use a three-inch bristle brush to apply two coats of Behr waterproof stain in dark brown. The bristle brush penetrates the wood, whereas spray painting simply sits on top of the wood.
>
> **B.** Because our carpenters use a bristle brush, your deck will be protected for 10 years—twice the minimum requirement.

The approach summary is an effective signpost for skimmers because it contains the key words about protecting a wood deck, and it successfully previews special tools. In the process section of this example, we've got information about who is doing the work and what tools we'll be using. This section also ghosts the competition by explaining how our method is superior to the spray painting approach our competitors may be pitching. In the benefits section, we connect the dots for the reader by explaining how our approach exceeds the minimum requirements—a clear strength. The government could copy and paste the last sentence into their source selection justification text.

The biggest difference between option two of the non-APB paragraphs and the APB version above is how easy it is to score the APB paragraph. Even if you knew nothing about wood decks, the APB structure clearly identifies the strengths. Written this way, you could easily select this proposal over a competitor's pitching a spray paint stain. We want to make it that easy for the government to pick your proposal against your competitors' proposals.

Now that I've explained what the APB model is, in the next part of this series I'll share how to indoctrinate this methodology in your team so that your content is consistently rated as *outstanding*.

Improving the quality of proposal content with the APB Writing Model – Part 3

Getting your team on board with APB

Julia Quigley

In the last two posts, I introduced the APB writing methodology to improve the quality of your proposal content and help reticent writers on your team. In this post, I wrap up the series by sharing some approaches to get your team on board and indoctrinate APB as the standard for all your proposals. How to get buy-in and commitment will vary depending on your context, but I've provided some general tips for implementation.

I recommend introducing the APB writing concept to the broadest group of people involved in your proposals as possible. Your writers and SMEs need to understand how to do what you're asking of them. Reviewers need to be aware of what you're asking the writers to do so they can have informed reviews. As you cover the APB principles, your reviewers will understand how to review proposals like evaluators do as you expose them to their scoring and benefits-focused mindset. Coordinators and editors will benefit from a session so they understand how they can support your mission within their roles.

A meeting with this broad of a group kickstarts the APB implementation process, setting a new standard across the board. A successful group meeting will facilitate discussion and a common understanding. After this meeting, you'll have the materials developed to indoctrinate proposal teammates from other companies and any new hires.

The key to learning is *saturation*, so you'll need to reinforce the concept again after the first meeting. In every kickoff meeting, review these writing standards with all participants. Setting the expectation at the beginning of the process gives you leverage to hold them accountable later in the process. It allows you to answer questions, and it brings any new team members into the fold.

Continue this practice, even if you have teammates from another company at your kickoff. You may feel like you're giving away the recipe to your *secret sauce*, but this information isn't proprietary to your company. Not sharing the APB method with teammates from the start weakens the proposal content and complicates your management of the bid. Whether your kickoff is internal only or includes teammates, be sure that everyone on the team understands the process and has handouts for future reference. A good handout will include a brief description of APB (feel free to take content from this series!) along with a clear example of APB from your company's materials.

As a final step, I recommend checking in with your writers individually prior to the first deadline so you can see their work and guide them if they're headed in the wrong direction. The process is time-consuming, but it's worth the investment for your team to have a positive and successful first experience with APB. In my experience, writers appreciate the structure of APB and return to it even when it isn't required because it makes writing so much easier.

Continue to review these writing standards in every kickoff, and use the APB language throughout reviews and debriefs until it becomes a part of your company's proposal culture.

Insights

Capture & Proposal Insights and Tips – Volume 3

Watch the APB Method Webinar Replay and download Webinar Slides (https://goo.gl/sWc5kL)

Editing to reduce proposal length

Writers should work within page budgets, but sometimes you need last-minute editing strategies to help shorten a document

Julia Quigley

At the end of the proposal lifecycle, we're all looking to cut page count—either to fall within the maximum page count or to increase readability with whitespace. While writers should adhere to page budgets early in the process to avoid last-minute stress, here are three quick editing tasks that will help decrease overall page count.

1. Remove nominalized verbs. Removing nominalized verbs saves space and makes writing easier to read.

Nominalization occurs when we turn a verb, adverb, or adjective into a noun. Proposals are typically littered with verbs turned into nouns. Nominalization isn't grammatically incorrect, but it clutters writing because nominalized verbs have to be paired with a true verb, thus doubling the number of words it takes to describe a simple action.

Does all this sound complicated, or give you flashbacks to elementary school? Don't worry, the principal is easy to understand with the following examples:

Nominalized phrase	Single-word replacement
We will *give an analysis*	We will *analyze*
We will *develop a solution*	We will *solve*
The board will *make a decision*	The board will *decide*
The administrator will *make an announcement*	The administrator will *announce*

People unknowingly resort to nominalized phrases when they're trying to elevate their speech or they aren't sure what to write. Unfortunately, nominalized phrases actually dilute the impact of writing. Find these phrases in your proposals and replace them with the appropriate verb, and you'll save space.

2. Replace passive voice with active voice. We often hear that we should avoid passive voice, but a lot of people aren't sure what passive voice is.

Passive voice occurs when the object of a sentence is made the subject of the sentence. The type of passive voice we see in proposals is when we say that something *has happened* or *will happen*, but we don't say by whom.

A classic example of this kind of passive voice is "the ball was thrown" or "the ball was thrown by Tim." Both say an action "was done"—a hallmark of passive voice—instead of saying "he did it." Re-written in active voice, the sentence is much shorter: "Tim threw the ball."

Passive voice is an easy trap to fall into with proposals; without a very clearly defined solution, writers are often unsure of who will be doing what on the project. As a result, proposals are bloated with sentences like the following:

Passive sentence	Active sentence
The quarterly report will be reviewed prior to submission to the COR.	The board will review the quarterly report prior to submission to the COR.
After the meeting, the notes will be distributed.	After the meeting, the PM will distribute the notes.
The meeting space will be reserved by the coordinator.	The coordinator will reserve meeting space.

Look for statements in your proposals that are missing who will do the work, and re-write them with an active construction to cut out several sentences worth of words. As a bonus, active sentences are easier for readers to remember, which increases the likelihood evaluators will remember key features of your proposal.

3. Eliminate paragraph "danglers." Look for paragraphs whose last line takes up 1/3 or less of the width of the page. Eliminating a few words anywhere in the paragraph will have a ripple effect that reduces the whole paragraph by one line. See the example below.

> In this paragraph, I've used more words than needed ~~to say what I want to say~~. That has resulted in a paragraph that is not only time-consuming to read, but ends with just a few words in the last line. With a little editing, this paragraph only takes up three lines.

Versus

> In this paragraph, I've used more words than needed. That has resulted in a paragraph that is not only time-consuming to read, but ends with just a few words in the last line. With a little editing, this paragraph takes up less lines.

Using this technique throughout the document will not only save you several lines of page count, but it can provide just enough space to put a table or graphic on a page where it couldn't previously fit, which multiplies the space-saving effect.

For example, if you have a table that extends to a second page, you'll waste page space because of the header repeating on the second page. If you eliminate a line or two of text earlier on the page, then the table fits on one page and there's no wasted space for the repeated header.

When applying these three principles in your editing process, edit at the sentence-level before looking for paragraph danglers or adjusting graphics and tables. Otherwise, the small reductions in words throughout the document will disrupt all the progress you made in desktop publishing.

Adding these techniques to your editing checklist will help you make room in your document and improve the quality of the writing you subject your evaluators to.

Increase audience engagement by varying your writing style

Varying sentence structure and length is key to maintaining reader interest

Julia Quigley

Do you ever get bored or even sleepy when reviewing a proposal? Have you ever found yourself at the bottom of a paragraph, but you can't recall what it said? I know I have.

If we feel that way, with only one proposal to read and a vested interest in improving the proposal, imagine how your customer feels. Your customer has stacks of proposals to assess. Further, many evaluators aren't directly invested in the resulting contract; they were just assigned to help get the evaluation done. Given these conditions, it's easy for reviewers to tune out.

The last thing we want to do is provide a poorly written proposal to evaluators whose attention is already slipping. We want to avoid monotonous writing that lulls readers to sleep like the rhythm of riding a train. Instead, we should achieve a writing style with bursts of speed, exciting turns, and pauses for reflection and absorption.

Two ways to engineer interest into our writing are sentence structure and sentence length.

Sentence structure

There are three basic types of sentence structures: simple, compound, and complex.

A **simple sentence** is an independent clause with a single subject and verb. "Our on-site team will develop the software" is a simple sentence.

A **compound sentence** is one sentence with two independent clauses combined by a coordinating conjunction (such as *and, for, but,* and others). For example, "Our on-site team will develop the software, and our remote team will test it" is a compound sentence.

A **complex sentence** has two clauses connected with a subordinating conjunction. Whereas in a compound sentence both clauses could stand on their own as simple sentences, in a complex sentence one clause wouldn't make sense as its own sentence. One clause is always subordinate to the other. For instance, "Our on-site team will develop the software before our remote team tests it" is a complex sentence. The independent clause "our on-site team will develop the software" could be its own sentence (as we saw above). The dependent clause "before our remote team tests it" can't stand as its own sentence.

Simple	Our on-site team will develop the software.
Compound	Our on-site team will develop the software, and our remote team will test it.
Complex	Our on-site team will develop the software before our remote team tests it.

Talking about dependent and independent clauses may sound like grammar gobbledygook, but it's important to recognize sentence structures so you can vary them in your writing. Too many simple sentences makes your writing choppy and juvenile, but too many compound or complex sentences decreases readability. To keep readers interested, find balance and variety of sentence structures in your writing.

Sentence length

In addition to sentence structure, consider the length of your sentences and how that affects the readability of your documents. When people aren't confident writers, they often resort to writing longer sentences with bigger words in an attempt to seem sophisticated. Unfortunately, this tactic actually makes writing harder to read.

The industry standard for professional writing is to aim for a 6th or 7th grade reading level. Writing at the 7th grade reading level doesn't mean your writing has to be boring or overly simple. In fact, Hemingway's classic *The Old Man and the Sea* is written at a 4th grade reading level! (Fun fact: this blog post is written at the 9th grade reading level).

Follow these instructions to determine the reading level of your document in Microsoft Word. If your reading level is too high, revise your writing so your average sentence length is about 20 words, and replace long words with shorter alternatives.

Applying these concepts

The real magic of reader engagement is the combination of variety in sentence structure *and* variety in sentence length. We tend to think of simple sentences as very short and complex sentences as very long (and complex!), but the opposite can be true for both. To illustrate, considering the following sentence:

Our on-site team of developers will build the XYZ software on ABC platform within 60 days in accordance with all regulations specified in

section 5.2 of the RFP and with the customer's SOP.

That sentence is 33 words long, but the sentence is still a simple sentence with only one subject. Similarly, the sentence below demonstrates how compound and complex sentences can be short and direct:

Our quality control board will review the monthly report before the PM submits it to the COR.

That complex sentence was only 17 words, nearly half the length of the simple sentence above.

As you revise your writing, look for ways to vary your sentence length and sentence structures. Don't worry about these principles on your first draft—it's more important at that stage to get your ideas organized on the page. As you refine the writing, look at each paragraph to assess the length of the sentences and how they are structured. If you find an especially long compound sentence, split it into two simple sentences with a good transition phrase. At the same time, don't be afraid of the occasional long sentence. The variety of short, long, simple, complex, and compound sentences will keep your reader engaged and attentive to the text.

Team

Management

Facing up to face time

Focusing on productive time rather than face time yields desired results

Lisa Pafe

Face time is defined as time that you spend at work especially in addition to your normal hours.

An extensive and often re-quoted 2006 study published in *Harvard Business Review* (https://goo.gl/L167Wj) declared the 40-hour work week dead and face time to be paramount. However, researchers warned that too much face time actually lowers productivity due to burn out and attrition.

In a more recent study published in *Human Relations* (https://goo.gl/W6sl9c), researchers conducted extensive interviews with 39 corporate managers. These managers reportedly perceived employees who put in more face time as more dedicated, hardworking, and responsible. These managers judged employees not based on productivity or results, but rather on ability to sit at their desk for more than 8 hours. Those efficient souls who completed their work in 8 hours or less were penalized. As Woody Allen said, 80% of success is just showing up!

It is interesting that even in this era of virtual work environments, being there is still paramount to gaining a reputation as a committed, responsible and dependable team player. Some team members are so worried about perceived face time, they spend hours each week just trying to be seen (in-person or online), all to the detriment of their work output (https://goo.gl/ODItaa).

Sadly, too many project and proposal managers focus on the showing up, rather than the results. I have experienced team dynamics where people are afraid to arrive after or leave before the boss. Often, they have finished their assignment and are pretending to look busy (but all they are really doing is checking their social media accounts). Even in virtual situations, we all tire of team members who constantly email into the wee hours of the morning, all to impress the manager with their commitment.

So how to counter face time? Some ideas:

1. Work with the team to agree on objective measures of work outputs and outcomes achieved.

2. Focus attention on the value each team member creates.
3. Reward results rather than hours logged.
4. Concentrate on productive time rather than face time in order to yield desired results.

Three lessons learned from a college homecoming weekend

Lisa Pafe

I recently spent Homecoming Weekend at my son's university. Many alumni attended. Over and over, I heard recent graduates tell their friends, "Don't ever graduate! The real world sucks!" It got me thinking…what is so great about college (besides the obvious) that we can apply to the workplace?

Engaging. College has a lot of fun activities that increase group engagement. Worldwide, only 13% of employees are engaged at work according to a recent Gallup poll (https://goo.gl/i09jPS). Why should you care? Because engaged employees generate 2.5 times the revenue than those who are not engaged. As a manager, you are responsible for an engagement strategy to get your team involved and performing. Engagement also increases retention, which in turn benefits the bottom line.

Bonding. As undergraduates, we find our group of friends, and they become friends for life. Of course, living, eating, socializing, and studying in close quarters enables bonding. Developing and maintaining close bonds in the workplace is an important element of managing effectively. Why? Research (https://goo.gl/484MpC) has shown that productivity and effectiveness increase when co-workers bond through team building, socializing, sharing lessons learned, and receiving and giving constructive feedback.

Parading. We attended a marvelous homecoming parade with floats, marching bands, candy tossers, cheerleaders, horses, and nice sports cars. Half time included all the pageantry of the homecoming court and the crowning of the king and queen. The entire stadium was one in shared happiness, pride, and sense of belonging. In the workplace, we often forget to celebrate and parade our team's accomplishments. Effective managers need to build in time to both revel in and display successes and wins.

My takeaway from the weekend is simple. If as managers, we can engage our employees, bond with our team, and parade our accomplishments, then perhaps our staff will return to visit their alma mater and shout, "The real world is a wonderful place!"

The single biggest communication problem – and how to fix it

Lisa Pafe

You talked. They listened. Soon enough it becomes clear that you talked, and they did not *hear* you. As George Bernard Shaw said, "The single biggest problem in communication is the illusion that it has taken place."

Project and proposal teams are melting pots. With the globalization of business, we face physical distances, clashing time zones, and a variety of cultural differences. Teams are comprised of individuals of different genders, generations, and native languages.

Studies have shown that people gravitate towards like-minded teammates, especially those with the same cultural background. The result is often that we fail to understand the words of those who we perceive as different.

Today, teams have the ability to communicate in so many ways—in-person, phone, text, email, chat, social media, and Web meetings—yet somehow the message is still garbled. With both verbal and non-verbal cues lost in translation, what can we do to truly connect? Here are 5 ideas.

1. **Create a communication plan.** The plan should address how you will communicate with teammates separated from you by distance, culture, gender, generational gaps, and the like. You don't necessarily need to publish this plan, but it is a good checklist to ensure you acknowledge and address differences.

2. **Learn cultural rules of behavior.** Understanding your customer or teammate's cultural values and norms is especially important if you are dealing with interactions across the globe. Do some research on how business people from that country handle business interactions and communications to avoid inadvertently offending your colleagues.

3. **Avoid jargon and acronyms.** Often we fall into the habit of using idioms, acronyms,

and/or complex terminology. Try speaking in plain English for greater clarity of intent.

4. **Embrace differences.** We learn and grow only by considering different viewpoints and continuously evolving our perspective. Exclusion of others through body language or overt action leads to poor organizational performance. Try to mix up your teams by pairing people of different backgrounds.

5. **Repeat, repeat, repeat.** When others talk, repeat what you think they said to gain confirmation. When you talk, ask each person to offer their perspective on what you just said. Or, at the end of a meeting or call, ask each attendee to summarize in writing the decisions and action items to ensure everyone is on the same page. By making everyone re-frame their understanding, you will gain greater precision.

Next time you meet, avoid the single greatest communication problem. Make sure communication has actually taken place.

5 ways to give thanks (without saying it)

Lisa Pafe

I had to chuckle at one of my favorite *Mad Men* episodes, "The Suitcase (https://goo.gl/1aJomk)." Peggy is miffed because Don is not being a thankful boss.

> **Don:** It's your job. I give you money, you give me ideas.
>
> **Peggy:** But you never say 'thank you.'
>
> **Don:** That's what the money is for.

It got me thinking of all the times that I have lamented that my boss or colleagues did not say thank you, and yes, I have been brought to tears, just like Peggy!

Receiving thanks is a form of credit and acknowledgement. Does it trump money? As the famous cosmetics titan Mary Kay Ash said, "There are two things people want more than sex and money: recognition and praise."

I do agree with Don Draper that we are being paid to do our jobs, so a thank you is not mandatory.

Sometimes, we actually thank colleagues too much, thus trivializing appreciation and making it more of a platitude. Thanks should be reserved only for accomplishments that go above and beyond. Here are five ways to say thank you without actually saying it.

1. **Share examples of good work in team meetings.** By discussing a specific success story and attributing it to the employee(s) responsible, you don't simply show you are thankful, you indicate that you admire and respect a job well done.

2. **Tell their boss.** Make sure to let the supervisor know that his/her employee has done an *above and beyond* job. You can tell them in person or send an email with a cc to the employee.

3. **Give formal public recognition.** This form of thanks, whether it be monetary or non-monetary, is very public and informs the rest of the team that you recognize and praise excellence.

4. **Provide flexibility.** If an employee shows a high level of performance excellence combined with responsibility and

reliability, allow them greater flexibility as a reward. This form of thanks can include letting them work remotely and/or enjoy flexible hours.

5. **Do something nice.** Rather than a verbal thanks, do something special for the high performer. This thank you could include having their car detailed while they are at work, inviting them to a meal with the boss, or providing a gift certificate for a massage.

Do not feel compelled to over-thank. Reserve verbal or non-verbal thanks for when such appreciation is truly deserved. In the end, it will mean a lot more.

Using confidence to lead

Three tactics to combat lack of confidence

Julia Quigley

I started working proposals for a small business directly out of graduate school with no knowledge of federal contracting and about 3 hours of on-the-job-training. Increasing the pressure, 4 months into the job I was managing proposals on my own after the only proposal manager left for extended maternity leave. Despite the odds, I became a successful, confident, and sought-after proposal manager.

During those first 2 years, I often had good reason to not feel confident, but I couldn't let that hinder my performance. I learned to rely on three tactics to combat those early difficulties:

1. Exude confidence even when I didn't feel like it.
2. Be confident, despite my ignorance.
3. Don't give up power in a conversation.

I was unfamiliar with proposals but was expected to manage them, so my confidence was naturally taxed. Initially, I undervalued the skills I accrued teaching writing as a graduate student at Texas State University. It took me a while to realize that managing a classroom, constructing an argument, and giving ad-hoc writing instruction weren't too far removed from facilitating proposal meetings, vetting a proposal solution, and coaching proposal writers. So long as I prepared as best as I could and spoke with conviction based on my transferable skills, I could exude confidence in meetings and interactions. The more I demonstrated that confidence in my interactions, the more consistent results I saw and the better my team worked with me.

Similarly, leadership expert Karin Hurt describes a woman who turned around a call center's customer service record by re-recording her greeting to radiate confidence and expertise (https://goo.gl/xfJ2y5). That recording initiated a transformation for her customers—they responded more positively to her throughout the call, and they expected her to deliver on her promise—which spurred her to prove them right. In the same way, as I practiced confidence with my proposal teams, I found myself working harder to keep up with my image.

Despite finding a wellspring of confidence in my prior experiences and learning to broadcast confidence, I was often faced with phrases, concepts, and problems I hadn't encountered before. I didn't always handle these situations with aplomb, but Scott Eblin's advice to "be confident in your ignorance" (https://goo.gl/v7mAbH) appropriately describes my most successful experiences. People respected my leadership when I honestly said I didn't know the answer and that I would come back to them with a response after I'd found time for reflection or research. Generally, people value honesty, preparation, and consistent follow-up above a leader faking it or skirting around the issue.

Finally, I learned how damaging it is to give up power with my words when I was unsure of a situation. In every conversation and meeting, I wielded power because of my title as proposal manager, but it was easy to lose that power when I wasn't feeling confident. Michael Hyatt identifies three ways we give up power in our conversations (https://goo.gl/9f6VG4):

1. We undermine our own authority with phrases like "I'm not expert, but…" or "I'm not prepared to speak on this, but…"

2. We hedge our statements with phrases like "I think" and "I suppose."

3. We give ourselves an out by saying "I'll try" or "I'll give it my best shot."

These words and others like them were quick to my lips when I wasn't confident about my perspective or course of action, but I quickly realized that by giving up power in these small, regular ways I lost the respect I needed to get people to rally behind my objectives.

In the end, I realized that lack of confidence only got in the way of using my skills to submit winning proposals. My teams followed my leadership best when I chose to exude confidence—even when confronted with my own ignorance—and when I used my words to conserve power I'd need later to get the job done.

Make fun a priority

Maryann Lesnick

As proposal professionals, we know the reality of hard work, long hours, deadlines, and stress. Members of the proposal team often have *day jobs,* too. Creativity, productivity, and contemplative abilities can be compromised by stress. The quality of our proposals can be compromised by stress.

According to a report from the American Institute of Stress, a non-profit dedicated to research and education on the subject, job pressures are the #1 cause of stress in the U.S., and 35% of Americans say their jobs are harming their physical or emotional health. Persistent stress can cause heart attacks, stroke, kidney disease, and rheumatoid arthritis. Stress is often caused by too many thoughts competing for your attention at the same time. Stress is what we feel when our lives or our jobs become overwhelming and too much for us.

There is a definite link between productivity and stress. We are less productive when we are stressed and more productive when we are not. In stimulating, positive, and happy environments, the team enjoys and excels at their work. A fun workplace and happy proposal team are not only more productive, but also more likely to produce a winning proposal.

Joy and laughter can bring us together in positive ways. Incorporating more fun and play into the work of your proposal team will improve the team's interactions, mood, and outlook. A positive mental attitude produces increased oxygen, endorphins, and blood flow to the brain, enabling us to think more clearly and creatively.

It's true what they say: laughter is the best medicine. Laughter is a powerful antidote to stress and conflict. Laughter makes you feel good. And that good feeling remains even after the laughter subsides. Play and laughter can keep your proposal team productive and motivated. It gives them a positive, optimistic outlook even when working on a proposal. Fun is attractive. We like to be around those who are having fun.

Here are suggestions for making the job of producing proposals more fun.

Don't be so serious all the time. It is possible to take yourself lightly and still be viewed as a competent and productive proposal manager. Fun and work do not have to be antonyms. Seek opportunities to interject humor with your proposal team. Show your human side and share fun things that are happening in your life. Remember that making the job fun helps the team to perform.

Smile! A smile is a curve that sets everything straight. Like laughter, smiles are contagious!

Give out compliments. Make it a habit to compliment someone on your team every day. Show your appreciation. Thank individuals for their contributions. Compliments make them feel good and make you feel good.

Put someone in charge of celebrating. Plan fun things to do to take a break during and after work. Celebrate milestones. Celebrate with a submission party and a win party. Celebrate the lessons learned on losses. Is anyone celebrating a birthday or work anniversary during the proposal period? Create some *happiness-boosting traditions* like bagels on Fridays or brownies on Wednesday afternoons. How about a lunch outing to go bowling or play mini-golf?

Add fun to your meetings. Bring in fun things like a Nerf ball to toss to the speaker in a brainstorming session. Start the meeting with a humorous story or joke. Add cartoons to your slides. Look for ways to bring fun into the process.

Collect and share your favorite funnies. Collect relevant comic strips or fun articles and hang them on your office door or in the war room.

Tell stories. Hold engaging and energetic solutioning sessions where you craft your solutions into a story that involves the customer and has a happy outcome. Create a compelling picture that tells the story. Bring erasable color markers and have some fun on the white board. Make everyone's job easier. Set clear objectives and realistic schedules. Avoid overtime and planned work on the weekends unless absolutely necessary.

Eliminate negativity. You can be the positive influence—the driver of positive thinking in the group. Be a cheerleader for success! Keep the glass half full! As the proposal manager, part of your job is to continually evaluate the morale of your team. If it's suffering, a break for fun can lift spirits, boost morale, and improve chances of success. Give your team opportunities to enjoy themselves. It will create a friendlier, happier, and all-around healthier environment for everyone.

Dale Carnegie said, "People rarely succeed unless they have fun in what they are doing."

Make fun a priority!

Lessons learned from the circus: building community for better teamwork

Julia Quigley

Everyone involved in a hobby or sport is a part of that activity's community. Those communities are sometimes known for certain characteristics—such as the dedication of runners or the intensity of CrossFit athletes. The circus is no different.

This post shares what you can learn from the circus community and how that community leads to better performance.

I've trained at several rigs in the United States and spoken with flyers from around the world who all attest to some common traits about circus communities:

1. **We fiercely support one another's successes.** I've never been in an environment that is as genuinely positive as circus is.

2. **We innovate together.** We enjoy trying new tricks and testing out new techniques. There's an element of playfulness that translates to innovations in our performances.

3. **We see ourselves as part of a team; collaboration is an essential component of our success.** For most performances, we literally could not perform without someone else's support. We rely on our fellow performers to accomplish our tricks, choreographers to showcase our talent, and rigging experts to keep us safe. Nobody is a one-man show.

The result is that we all feel powerful and comfortable excelling. We're not worried about jealousy or making a mistake while being creative. We try more and do more.

When you reflect on prior positions you've held, you can probably recall working on teams that did not support one another; teams where everyone was looking out for their own self-interest and covering their backs. On the other hand, you may also recall being a part of teams with a great sense of community that helped you cope with challenges and excel. I've experienced both professionally, and the teams with a sense of community were not only more pleasant to work with, I felt empowered to grow my professional skills and comfortable trying out new techniques.

The *Harvard Business Review* also recognizes the value of collaboration. In "Eight Ways to Build Collaborative Teams," Lynda Gratton and Tamara J. Erickson studied 15 multinational corporations to determine the top eight characteristics of successfully collaborative groups. Below are the three characteristics most relevant to our discussion:

1. First, in most successful collaborative teams, 20–40% of team members already knew each other. When part of the team shared a history, team formation sped up and the group achieved results faster.

2. Second, they found that clear roles were more important for collaboration than a clear plan. People perform the best when they know how they should function with the group and what their area of responsibility is. When people understand their roles and what they are responsible

for, they willingly participate in a plan or create one to fulfill their role.

3. Third, leaders of the most successful groups were task oriented *and* relationship oriented. There's long been debate about which type of leader is more effective, but when it comes to collaboration, they need to build relationships and keep everyone accountable to the tasks required to complete the project.

Based on the *Harvard Business Review's* research and my experiences with circus, I have four recommendations for building better proposal communities:

1. **Build proposal-responsible teams that combine new and familiar people.** Even though you'll constantly be working in new groups because of different teaming arrangements and availability of internal resources, you can increase your team's effectiveness by making sure at least 20% of the team has worked together before. They'll feel more comfortable asking one another for help, and they'll demonstrate

successful norms you established on the last proposal they worked together.

2. **Don't just administer tasks; build relationships on the team and innovate together**. If you can't build rapport around small talk or common interests, take time to talk with team members individually about their thoughts on the proposals and their stresses in the office, and try to innovate some new process improvements. Listening to their perspectives will go a long way in relationship building.

3. **Clearly define roles and responsibilities on your team.** A good time to do this is at kickoff. Don't just introduce people based on their roles in this project, explain what each of those roles is responsible for. This sets a common standard and allows you to keep them accountable to those standards.

4. **Keep your team engaged after submission.** Your project may be "completed," but if you want to foster a sense of community around proposals, then you should keep the team updated on the award outcome and any valuable information from the

source selection. This should be a part of every company's standard operation procedure (SOP) for lessons learned, but it is often overlooked. If you don't keep your team updated on the outcomes of their hard work, they won't be motivated to help on the next project.

What steps will you take to improve community at your office?

Lessons learned from the circus: how to handle mistakes

There's more truth than jest to the saying that a proposal submission is a bit like a circus. Learn from professional performers how to handle mistakes.

Julia Quigley

As a hobbyist trapeze artist, I can attest the truth in jokes about managing proposals being like running a circus. Yes, it's a juggling act with multiple performers dancing in and out of each other's paths. But a circus performance and a proposal submission have deeper traits in common.

For instance, both activities are team efforts with defined roles and responsibilities. The teams comprise members with varied backgrounds. In proposal development, you may work with team members from different departments, of different ages, and with different levels of experience. In my trapeze classes, I also work in teams with varying levels of experience, different ages, and different abilities.

Another commonality is the pressure to succeed. There is a lot on the line in proposals and in a circus! In trapeze, we face the success or failure of a performance, but we also have each other's lives in our hands. While you might not have your colleagues' lives in your hands, there's a lot on the line in proposal development too—the company profits, the possibility of a bonus, our very careers as well as those of our colleagues.

In the end, whether you're in a circus performance or working on a proposal, you are performing in a discrete role on a diverse team with a lot on the line.

With these commonalities, there's a lot you can learn from the circus community about handling mistakes, consistently succeeding, and building community.

Handling mistakes: what we experience

With so much on the line in proposals, the climate is tense and sometimes explosive when someone on the team makes a big mistake. I have seen people miss major compliance items and miss deadlines. Early in my career, I made a mistake with the pricer that potentially revealed proprietary pricing information to a major competitor! To say the president of the company was upset is an understatement. I left his office ashamed, and while I never made that mistake (or one like it) again, my anxiety about all things proposal increased substantially.

Handling mistakes in the circus

In circus, mistakes are handled a little differently from what I experienced above.

First, success and failure are both recognized as a team effort. If a performer fails in her part of the performance, the blame isn't immediately assigned to the performer. Everyone involved assesses their own performance to determine if they contributed to the performer's failure. If there are any discrepancies, the head coach who observes the entire operation has the final say.

The most notable characteristic is that mistakes aren't punished; they are discussed, understood, and improved upon. Everyone involved understands the high risks involved. In fact, making a mistake is unnerving because you realize how close you are to injury at any given moment. No one is going to add anger on top of fear. Instead, the group assesses the cause and does better next time.

Research on handling mistakes

This last point about not punishing mistakes is echoed by the *Harvard Business Review* (HRB). In an article titled "Why Compassion is a Better Managerial Tactic than Toughness," the authors found that compassionate responses increase loyalty and trust.

When someone makes a professional mistake, they are vulnerable. If you work with good employees, they will feel awful for making the mistake. When a coworker or manager responds compassionately, the employee begins to trust his coworker and build loyalty with the company. However, angry responses cause the employee to disengage and decreases trust.

In fact, angry responses decrease creativity in the office. Creativity usually involves risk, and employees who fear angry responses to failure are less likely to try creative approaches to their work. Not only is anger counter-productive, it doesn't contribute to a positive reputation. People who react to mistakes with anger are seen as powerful, but ineffective.

Changing how we respond to mistakes in proposals

If you aren't already, I recommend conducting proposal reviews with a reviewer's caucus and debriefing writers on the outcome. Most organizations default to gathering the reviewers and writers in a room and reviewing the comments, but this can be confusing and demoralizing for the writers—especially if the reviewers don't agree.

Instead, take a cue from the circus. Designate a single point of authority, schedule a meeting with just the reviewers, and determine a consensus that the single point of authority will relay to the writers.

Second, stop perpetuating the idea that one role on the team is responsible for wins. The reality is that proposals are a team effort, so wins and losses are the result of a team effort.

One company I worked for posted the cover of every winning proposal on a wall, signed by the proposal manager. On the positive side, this practice was a way to congratulate each other's successes. On the other hand, this approach made it seem like any win was the proposal manager's win, when it was really a team win. This practice exemplifies some of our habits and ways of discussing proposals that contribute to the unfair idea that a win rests on one person's shoulders.

My final recommendation is to accept responsibility for your mistakes instead of trying to hide them. Hiding mistakes usually stems from fear of judgment from your colleagues or your own internal judgment. Instead of hiding, show yourself some of the compassion the *Harvard Business Review* article advocated. By acknowledging your mistakes up front, you're contributing to a new culture in your workplace where mistakes happen and people move on.

Your takeaways

What other applications can you come up with for handling mistakes better?

Lessons learned from the circus: consistently succeeding

Julia Quigley

Several years ago, a performer at Cirque Du Soleil died during a performance because of a mistake in her rigging. This was newsworthy not just because of the tragedy, but because this was the first time a Cirque Du Soleil performer died during an act, despite the death-defying, acrobatic feats that fill their show. Everyone involved in a circus performance works diligently to have a successful performance, free from mistakes.

While the mistakes we make as proposal professionals may not cost us our lives, there's certainly a lot on the line. From circus performers, we can learn the importance of communication and adaptability to succeeding consistently.

Communication is critical in collaborative projects like trapeze and other circus performances. Acrobats and aerialists have to communicate about what is working and what's not in real time in order to succeed. Sometimes people are afraid to express their needs because they think it will come across as a criticism or that they'll seem "needy," but circus performers quickly realize that communicating your needs is the only way to improve. Unless you tell your partner that you need more or less lift, for instance, they can't know how to help you into position.

Circus performers also have to adapt to new environments and new partners. An aerialist on the flying trapeze could perform her best trick with a new catcher and miss the catch because of the new dynamics. The catcher could be shorter than the last catcher she trained with, which means she might need to travel a bit more to reach him, or he might need to adjust the timing of his catch. Failing on the trick with a new partner doesn't necessarily mean anyone did anything "wrong"—it just means they need to adapt to be successful in this new dynamic.

Research also supports the premise that communication and adaptability are essential for team success. In their book *Beyond Performance: How Great Organizations Build Ultimate Competitive Advantage* authors Scott Keller and Colin Price write, "Organizational health is about adapting to the present and shaping the future faster and better than the competition." They emphasize the importance of adapting and changing well together as a team, which is impossible without good communication skills.

Leadership expert Karin Hurt shares seven questions to improve communication. She recommends asking your team the following:

1. What is working and what's not working about your communication practices? This creates a baseline for future communication.

2. Who are our stakeholders and what do they care about?

3. What additional information do you need from me?

4. How will we use email?

5. When will we meet by person, phone, web conference, etc.? People enter groups with their own assumptions about protocol for online communication and meetings, so discussing these expectations and setting a standard prevents unintended chafing.

6. How will we ensure our meetings are effective?

7. How will we resolve conflict? Once you have consensus about how to handle conflict, people can address concerns without anxiety about the appropriate course of action. Those involved in the conflict are less likely to be aggravated when they approved of the conflict resolution approach.

Based on the resounding importance of communication and adaptability, I offer three recommendations.

1. **Discuss communication strategies during proposal kickoff.** Every time you work on a proposal, you're working with a new collaborative team. Using some of Karin Hurt's questions during kickoff can help build a sense of community in your team and improve the ability of your team to communicate well. If you can communicate well, there's less of a chance your team will make a mistake, and you increase your ability to adapt to all the changes that happen during a proposal.

2. **No matter what your role on the proposal is, learn to express what you need for success on the project.** If proposal team members aren't providing you what you need for success, don't be afraid to tell them specifically what you need and how it affects the project. The request isn't inherently a criticism and it doesn't make you needy; it's direct communication.

3. **Be flexible as you work with different proposal teams/team members.** Even if you think you have your process down pat, you'll work with colleagues and customers who have different needs and expectations that you need to adapt to. Remember, adaptability is a part of organizational health that makes teams successful and competitive. Adapting doesn't mean you were doing something wrong before; it just means you have to change to be successful in this environment.

Beyond these tips, how are you going to embody this circus "lessons learned" with adaptation and communication?

Being Productive

Capture and proposal innovations: time management

Lisa Pafe

Time. As capture and proposal professionals, we find that it is most certainly NOT on our side. We are always battling time constraints and deadlines that fall at the most inconvenient times, such as vacations or family events. Summer is particularly taxing, especially as we get closer to the end of the federal fiscal year and the government pushes out a seemingly endless stream of solicitations.

Advice abounds on how to better manage time. What time management innovations are really most useful for our profession?

People

The biggest time waster related to people is due in large part to distractions caused by innovation. Our teams are so connected to the world through smart phones, tablets, iPads, and the like that they lack focus. It is virtually impossible to hold a meeting without most of the attendees checking their email, social media posts, and text messages.

With all the innovations in personal applications, your team members may even be turning off their oven or spying on their nanny. The problem is not so much a lack of time, but a lack of focus.

The best way to gain focus is to demand focus. Urge the team to focus on winning, not on tweeting. This focus involves breaking bad habits like constantly checking email. When planning short meetings, require attendees to pay attention, and for longer meetings, schedule breaks for checking messages. Do not feel guilty for demanding focus because it is quite likely that the majority of the distractions have nothing to do with the meeting agenda.

"Starting each day by focusing on winning reminds us of where and how we should be spending our time. It also makes it easier to resist the urge to respond to distractions that might seem important but really aren't. When we manage our distractions instead of letting them manage us, we have a lot more time to accomplish the things we need to do in order to win." –Holly G. Green, CEO, The Human Factor

Time management processes

Innovative capture and proposal managers borrow from best-practice methodologies such as the Capability Maturity Model Integration (CMMI), the Project Management Institute (PMI) Project Management Body of Knowledge (PMBOK), and the International Organization for Standardization (ISO).

These methodologies all herald the importance of repeatable processes as a means to make the most of our time. It is true that repeatable processes reduce errors and rework. However, often we blindly follow a capture or proposal process that was once innovative but has become nothing more than a habit. Some habits are bad habits that we need to eliminate.

For example, some companies follow a solutioning process that takes them down a time-wasting path of building storyboards to the subtask level.

They get so focused on filling in the multitude of boxes in the storyboards that they forget to solution the value proposition. The result is very repetitive features, benefits, and proofs text that is of little help to the writers. Blindly focusing on a process rather than creating a winning solution is a bad habit.

Another example relates to meetings. Often we try to be inclusive. We add so many participants to our meeting invitations that our meetings (kickoff, tag-ups, color team reviews) become unwieldy. It wastes the capture or proposal manager's time to manage an overly large meeting with too many talking heads. In addition, all of the individuals who are not really needed are wasting their time. Meetings come with an opportunity cost. Only those who must be there should be there.

Examine your processes. Are some of them bad habits? Which ones can you eliminate or revise?

Technology: There's an app for that!

Time management apps that you can download to your smartphone, laptop, or tablet abound. All have free versions as well as paid versions with greater functionality. My favorite? The Komorian Eternity Time Log for iPhone or iPad has features such as the ability to define and time personal and work activities, review time logs and calendars, run detailed reports and pie charts, back up data, and export results to fully analyze how you spend your time—and thus gain greater productivity. Similar highly rated apps include HoursTracker, My Hours, Eternity Time Log, and aTimeLogger. An APMP publication referenced a list of free time management apps perfect for business including Toggl, My Minutes, RescueTime, and Paymo. Options abound.

Use time management apps to your best advantage. Can you leverage technology to analyze your time, eliminate time wasters, get more productive, and have more hours in the day for your personal life?

People, processes, and technology innovations can save time or be time wasters. Be sure that you understand the difference.

Reprinted by permission from the *APMP-NCA Executive Summary.*

5 strategies to get your team performing...and winning

Lisa Pafe

Productivity is getting maximum results for time and effort expended. For business development, capture, and proposal professionals, maximum results provide a greater number of qualified bids and/or bid-related activities, increased quality, and decreased error (non-compliance)—all resulting in more wins. Yet most companies are content with a win rate of no more than 50%.

On one of my favorite *Mad Men* episodes, aptly named "Commissions and Fees", Don Draper says "You're happy with 50%? …I won't settle for 50% of anything. I want 100%." Clearly, we can't achieve a 100% win rate except perhaps in our dreams, but we can expect and demand 100% productivity.

Everyone is facing tight budgets and more and more competition. We simply cannot afford unproductive teams that decrease our win probability, waste time and money, and result in proposal losses. Educator and psychologist Bruce Tuckman defined the five stages that all teams experience: Forming, Storming, Norming, Performing, and Adjourning (https://goo.gl/z1pUvX).

Yet, there is no guarantee that you will ever reach the performing (productive) stage. Research shows that at least 3/5 of team time is spent forming and storming. So in a relatively short amount of time (most proposal turnaround times are 10 to 60 days), we spend most of the time getting to know each other and fighting before we get around to working well and performing. In response, I have developed five strategies to move my teams more rapidly from forming and storming to the performing stage.

1. **Extreme clarity.** Define success in clear terms. Success equals winning. Confront difficult issues by focusing on clarity. Agree on meaningful objectives.

2. **Continuous communications.** Continuously take the pulse of the team. Ask and answer questions in a group setting as well as one-on-one.

3. **Coaching, coaching, coaching.** Ask what have you done (NOT what will you do). Use well-timed praise and criticisms. Evaluate work in progress and make continuous corrections. Meet one-on-one to coach on constructive team behavior.

4. **Agility.** Borrowed from Agile iterations in software development. Resolve conflicts as they emerge; do not let them linger. Review work in smaller chunks to proactively address problems or to distribute good work as an example.

5. **Circumvent when necessary.** Avoid being defensive or blaming. However, some people are not meant to be team members; circumvent by either having them work alone or dismissing them from the team.

These five strategies will help you avoid common pitfalls that disrupt team productivity and encourage your team to want and win more than 50%.

3 meeting management best practices

Save time and build credibility by scheduling meetings only when discussion is required

Julia Quigley

Meetings are essential in business and proposals, but they also waste a lot of time. We groan about the weekly proposal staff meeting because it takes away from productive time at our desks. Meetings from corporate and HR are unnecessarily long, leaving you wishing that you'd skipped each and asked a coworker to fill you in. Then there are those meaningful meetings you're anticipating—like the strategy and solution sessions—but when there's no follow-up after the meeting, ideas dissipate and you end up repeating conversations and decisions. Or worse, immediately after the meeting you realize that you and your colleagues walked away with very different impressions of what happened in the meeting, nullifying any progress you thought you'd made.

While we've all bemoaned these kinds of ineffective meetings, sometimes we perpetuate these issues when we're the meeting leader. We can save everyone some time and build credibility in our organizations by scheduling meetings only when discussion is required, inviting the right people, and guiding meeting attendees before and after the meeting.

Only schedule meetings when discussion is required

In "How to Stop Having Stupid Staff Meetings," Karin Hurt makes it clear that meetings should only be scheduled when a discussion needs to take place. Relaying information is best handled through other forms of communication, such as email blasts, newsletters, or updates to a shared portal/document repository. For staff meetings in particular, Hurt suggests tossing the typical round-robin report format and instead asking questions that generate conversation.

If you currently host a regular proposal department status meeting, consider replacing it with 10- or 15-minute one-on-ones with your staff. If you have important information to relay to the team, you can send a group email prior to the individual meetings so you can address questions during the individual sessions.

Similarly, we can apply this concept to handling proposal amendments. When an RFP amendment is released, don't automatically schedule a meeting to review the changes with the entire team. Determine if the requirement changes are so direct and straightforward that you could send out a detailed email update or talk with one or two people directly. Only schedule the meeting if the updated requirements warrant a discussion among multiple proposal project team members.

Schedule the right people

When scheduling a meeting, be conscious of who needs to attend the meeting versus who needs to be kept informed of meeting outcomes. Some attendees just need to be briefed on specific outcomes of the meeting, and being present for the entire meeting wastes their time and diminishes the collective energy and attention in the room. Smaller meetings are easier to manage, and you'll establish a reputation in the office as someone who only sends invitations to meaningful meetings.

The following rule of thumb for determining the right number of meeting attendees comes from the

Harvard Business Review's recent article on having better meetings:

- 8 or fewer attendees for decision-making.
- 18 or fewer attendees for brainstorming.
- 1,800 or fewer attendees for rallying the troops.

Lead your attendees before and after the meeting

Get the most out of your meetings by guiding your attendees before and after the meeting. *Harvard Business Review's* suggested agenda templates include a section for how meeting attendees can prepare for that segment of the agenda. This practice guides attendees in case they aren't experienced, and it demonstrates your expectation that attendees will be prepared.

To illustrate this concept in practice, for a proposal kickoff meeting you may list which sections of the RFP attendees should review prior to the meeting. This makes it clear to attendees that you do expect them to read those sections and makes it easy for them to find relevant information. The preparation for a kickoff meeting may seem obvious to you, but listing everything on the agenda helps orient attendees who are new to proposals, and it allows you to hold people accountable to the standards you established.

In addition to setting your attendees up for success, follow up with attendees to guide their post-meeting actions. In "3 Communication Mistakes Screwing Up Teamwork," Karin Hurt implicates poor meeting follow-up as a major cause in team communication breakdowns. She recommends concluding each meeting with a summary of key takeaways and action items. This wrap-up provides traction for any next steps and clarifies the discussion.

Meetings are necessary, but they don't necessarily have to waste time. You'll have more-effective meetings if you limit meetings to discussions instead of reporting, invite the right people, and guide your attendees before and after meetings.

Bad processes or bad habits?

Lisa Pafe

How do we know whether we have bad processes or bad habits?

According to the *Merriam Webster Dictionary*:

Process: *a series of actions that produce something or that lead to a particular result.*

Habit: *a usual way of behaving: something that a person does often in a regular and repeated way*

We often follow processes—whether for acquiring new business, managing a project or proposal, or retaining customers—that are based on *proven processes*. The particular result we seek varies, but in general we seek a successful outcome.

Yet even when results are empirically poor, we often continue to do things the same way. For example, perhaps we are chasing new business, and we follow our best-practice business development processes. The result is a downward trend in win rates. While we may hold a lessons-learned session or attend a debrief meeting with the customer to learn why, often we fail to isolate the problem and then revise our processes accordingly. In many cases, we do not even bother to find out why we failed; we just keep on keeping on!

Another example relates to our health. Perhaps we work long hours at our desk without interruption, snacking on unhealthy foods and sleeping poorly at night. Our work quality suffers, but we repeat the bad habits thinking that hours equate to results—or at least the face time (https://goo.gl/zqmlqu) will impress the boss.

When we consistently obtain poor results, the bad process is the same as a bad habit. Bad habits are really a combination of laziness and inability to accept change. We can blame the bad habit on the bad processes—"that's the way we do it"—or we can isolate the root of the problem and determine what needs to change.

So, ask yourself the following questions:

1. Does the process yield the results we desire?

2. Is there any reason to continue the process?

If the answer to both questions is no, then it is time to change the process or processes that have become bad habits. The change may cause stress in the short term, but it may also result in better outcomes. If not, then repeat the two questions above and continuing changing.

Using "Send Personally" in business development and proposals

The right tool can save you precious time—and Send Personally is a hidden gem to save time when composing emails

Julia Quigley

Technology has increased the capacity for what we can do in proposals, but with the plethora of new tech coming out, it's hard to keep up and sometimes great products fail to garner national attention. In this post, I'm featuring one application that isn't widely known, but could save you time in business development (BD) and proposals.

Send Personally, a plug-in for Microsoft Outlook, allows you to compose one email with several recipients in the "To" field and Outlook will send an individual version of that message to everyone in the "To" field. For instance, you could write an email about an upcoming deadline to John, Sally, and David. When you click "Send Personally," Outlook will send three identical emails: one each to John, Sally, and David.

If you want to add a personal touch, you can set the email to include a greeting with the name associated with the email address, so that John's email will greet John and Sally's email will greet Sally. There are a few other ways to customize your greeting, based on the name of your distribution list or a user name associated with the email address. Since I downloaded Send Personally, I've identified several tasks it will help me complete more efficiently. Here are a few ideas for how you might use it to save time in BD and proposal management.

- In BD, you could use this tool to prospect with potential clients. For instance, you could craft a message about your company's IT capabilities tailored for an Army audience, list several potential Army customers in the "To" field, select a custom greeting, and hit "Send Personally." Each potential customer would receive your email with the customized greeting without knowing it was sent to others as well.

- You could also use Send Personally when vetting potential partners for an opportunity. If you have data calls that each company needs to complete, you can compose a message explaining how to complete the forms and what the deadline is and "Send Personally" to each company without revealing your other potential partners.
- As a proposal manager, you might use Send Personally when notifying a writer of a late submission. Generally, your writers know one another so there's no need for anonymity that prevents you from a mass email, but using "Send Personally" could help you apply a little pressure. When contributors see that they are part of a group that missed a deadline, there's a sense of relief that "I'm not the only one." That relief lessens the urgency to submit their materials. By crafting a polite but firm reminder of the missed deadline and clicking "Send Personally," each person will feel the pressure of your personal attention without your taking the time to craft individual emails.

Insights

Capture & Proposal Insights and Tips – Volume 3

The Proposal Doctor

Ask the Proposal Doctor

Creating balance between "required" and "desired"?

Dear Proposal Doctor,

Senior executives in my organization are constantly inserting material into the proposal that is not called for in the RFP and spending time on proposal components that don't get evaluated separately.

The executive summary eats up hours of everyone's time, and even if it is sometimes required, it is almost never evaluated. Likewise, the graphics are time-consuming and expensive to conceptualize, render, revise, and review. Over and over again. Every major section has an introduction that is not required.

We are adding so much to an already difficult workload, and the required sections that do get scored are going to suffer. How can I scale this back before it kills us all?

–Drowning

Dear Drowning,

You didn't indicate what kind of RFPs you are responding to, but I can make an educated guess that they are Federal Government RFPs. The reason that people want to add sections and introductions and graphics is that often government RFPs are not structured in a way that lets companies sell effectively. They are structured so that it will be easy to line the proposals up and compare them. So, there is a natural tension between what the RFP calls for and how your colleagues want to present the solution.

It is also important to remember that just because something doesn't get scored, it doesn't mean that it does not create an impression. This is particularly true for graphics. I have only heard of one instance when a specific graphic was identified as the reason why a company's proposal was scored in a particular way, but I strongly believe that graphics indirectly influence all evaluators.

As a proposal manager, you need to watch the balance between what is *required* by the customer and what is *desired* by the executives very carefully. If you already have a process to ensure responsiveness to the items that are required and specifically evaluated, good graphics can increase your win probability. An executive summary, likewise, even if it is not evaluated, can be helpful because it forces the team to condense and refine the main messages of the document.

At the same time, you cannot afford to neglect the mandatory items. Sometimes it makes sense to assign a small team to the required items and make sure that is all they focus on. If you explain this logically to your executive team, I am sure they will understand. You might even want to color code each section in your outline so that it is clear to everyone what is going to be scored. Also, whenever possible, try to take the *desired* sections or ideas and make them subordinate to the ones that are *required*.

All the best,

The Proposal Doctor (Wendy Frieman)

Ask the Proposal Doctor

How to bring proposal solutioning to closure?

Dear Proposal Doctor,

My team has been locked in a room for the better part of a week with instructions to stay there until they, that is, we, have created a solution for an upcoming proposal. We don't have a draft RFP to work from, but we have an outdated statement of work (SOW). Everyone has a different idea as to how to build the solution, and the discussion meanders with no end in sight.

Although everyone involved is intelligent as well as competent, something is missing from this team, or we would have what we need by now. Without a solution, we cannot bid.

As a lowly proposal manager, surrounded by people more technically knowledgeable than I am, how can I bring this process to closure?

–In Solution Hell

Dear In Solution,

First of all, you are not in hell (for which there are different exit strategies), but in purgatory. Although you gave no clues as to your customer and your business area, I can definitely discern one feature of your team—it lacks a leader. Often, that role has to be filled by the proposal manager, but not if you consider yourself *lowly*, so please, for all our sakes, shake that attitude and take pride in a profession that has high standards and demands respect.

I want to address your situation at two levels: process and content. For the process, you need someone who can facilitate the discussion with the goal of arriving at decisions. Facilitation is a skill as well as an art form. Is there anyone in your organization outside the team who can play this role? It is worth identifying the good facilitators, because we need them to not only help create solutions, but also to achieve consensus, analyze lessons learned, and assist in other proposal-related processes where emotions tend to run high and the threat of deadlock looms. If all else fails, you need to learn facilitation skills yourself. There are courses and books that can help, but the most important learning device is practice.

For the content, I would start with a clear definition. Back in the Cold War, when the U.S. and the Soviets started to debate arms control treaties, the talks almost collapsed because the Soviets would not agree to any form of verification. Then one of the negotiators asked each side to define verification, only to find that that the Soviets were objecting to something that the U.S. was not demanding in the first place. Each side was using a different definition of the term.

A solution can be anything, so it is especially important to apply definitions in this context. Are you talking about a process, a product, a team of people, or a system? Definition is the first step.

Another concept that can be helpful is *simplicity*. I have managed proposals where the essence of the solution was a highly customized MS Excel workbook. It doesn't have to be elaborate; it has to be effective at the right price point and solve the customer's problem.

One way to get at the solution is to ask the staff you are proposing how they plan to do the work. A good proposal is a plan for running the program, and if no one knows how the work will be performed, it is worth asking whether it makes sense to bid.

Finally, don't start with a blank piece of paper. "Good artists copy; great artists steal." One book that is an excellent repository of solution ideas is Vijay Kumar's *101 Design Methods: A Structured Approach for Driving Innovation in Your Organization*.

The need to break this stalemate is a wonderful opportunity for you to build new skills, show leadership, and enhance the respect people have for you and for our profession. I know you can meet this challenge!

All the best,

The Proposal Doctor

Ask the Proposal Doctor

Eliminate daily standup meetings?

Dear Proposal Doctor,

My capture manager and solution architect are tired of the daily standup meeting and want to discontinue it. Others are grumbling as well. In fact, I can't prove that it is efficient or that it adds value. I want to continue it, because that is how I was taught to manage proposals, but it is an uphill battle. What is your advice?

–Fighting the Good Fight

Dear Fighting,

Yes, the daily standup is part of the holy grail of our business. For a good reason! Every time I have been persuaded to discontinue this activity, and it has only happened rarely, the proposal has gone off the rails. Those who want to discontinue it usually assume that, as one person put it, "We are all talking to each other all day anyway." Often that is not the case.

From where I sit, the call is essential and I insist on it, with the proviso that any individual call might get canceled if there is a genuine proposal emergency. (For example, the capture manager has been kidnapped by aliens.) The daily discipline pays off in the long run, even if it is hard to point to the value of any particular call. Concert pianists, athletes, writers, and soldiers all have daily rituals that are part of achieving greatness in their profession. Ours is no different.

Here are some tips to make the call more palatable.

- Keep it short. I limit mine to 15 minutes, but if I end early I have some minutes in the bank that I can use in case I need a couple of extra minutes at a later meeting.
- Use a standard agenda so people know what to expect.
- Impart something new to the team at every meeting. Every 24 hours in a proposal, events occur that are of interest to the team. If there is nothing new from the customer, maybe there is a newspaper article about the competition. Maybe there is a weather or traffic announcement everyone needs to know about. Unless your proposal goes on

for years, it should not be too hard to find something of value.

Keep fighting the good fight. The payoff is worth it.

All the best,

The Proposal Doctor

Ask the Proposal Doctor

Best way to get new proposal managers up to speed

Training for proposal managers is a tricky business

Dear Proposal Doctor,

I have just assumed a position as director of a team of junior proposal managers. They are bright and they have great work habits, but they have only minimal training and not much experience.

What is the best way to get them up to speed? By the end of the year, they will each need to be able to independently manage several concurrent task order proposals ranging from 25-50 pages (for the technical and management sections).

Thanks very much,

–The New Director

Dear New Director,

Congratulations on your new position. Training for proposal managers is a tricky business because so much of what these young people need to know is specific to your company and your industry. Moreover, there are many different ways of approaching this challenge.

I like to think about three broad categories in which proposal managers need to develop, and you have to be the judge of the right mix. First, they need to know the terminology, skills, and concepts (color reviews, compliance matrices, and the like). Second, they need a certain amount of subject matter knowledge relevant to your industry. One does not have to be a civil engineer to manage a proposal to build a bridge, but it certainly helps to be familiar with construction contracting as opposed to IT service contracts. Third, all proposal managers need a certain level of leadership and facilitation skills.

The real challenge is getting each type of training. APMP (https://goo.gl/4GMrfz) and other professional organizations offer training on proposal terminology and concepts. Classroom learning is necessary, but not sufficient. Your team needs a way to practice implementing those concepts in a safe environment, when life does not hang in the balance. One option is to ask them to prepare and use a compliance matrix at the pink team stage, when there is time to adjust for error. Another is to ask them to serve as second in command to a red or pink team facilitator. Subject matter training is probably the easiest one to tackle, because you can look to whatever courses or seminars you use for new hires, particularly new hires fresh out of school with no industry background. Leadership skills can be gained in many different ways, but I would recommend not relying on books or formal coursework for this. Mentoring, shadowing, and direct feedback from senior professionals are all likely to prove more useful as long as you incorporate them into a formal program and don't rely on ad-hoc comments, which might be neither well delivered nor well received.

In general, I think it is safe to say that the easier the solution sounds (send someone to a *boot camp*, sign someone up for an online course, give someone a *how-to* book), the less useful it is likely to be. Training for this profession is inherently hands-on and interactive.

Whatever you do, set measurable goals and track the progress of the team. Otherwise, training and education objectives can seem nebulous. A colleague once told me that in golf, "If you're not keeping score, you're just practicing." I think this really applies to many other endeavors.

All the best,

The Proposal Doctor

Ask the Proposal Doctor

Focusing on proposal priorities, not on fires?

Dear Proposal Doctor,

How can I be sure that I am spending my time in the best way possible when I seem to spend all day responding to crises?

If a company is about to jump off the team, I have to deal with that right away. If my best writer just landed in the hospital, I have to replace that person right away. If files are lost, I have to get to the root cause and fix our version control process.

So many things happen in the course of the day. There are so many fires to put out. It's hard to stay focused on what is truly important. Is there a methodology for organizing time on a proposal?

–The Fireman

Dear Fireman,

This is a great question, and a difficult one. We can't manufacture more hours in the day, so allocation and best use of each hour is critical.

Methodologies exist for this, of course. The problem is implementing them on a regular basis. If it takes 2 hours to figure out how to save 2 hours, we end up back where we started. So, I would recommend the following simple steps.

First, make sure the items that must get done each day from your perspective are documented in some kind of system—paper, electronic, white board, or whatever works. Second, make sure your calendar is up to date with all commitments that are tied to a particular time. Third, take 20 minutes a day to step back and review your action items and your calendar for the next day.

Do it in a place where you are not distracted, and make sure you have your list and calendar in front of you. Make notes about your priorities for the next 24 hours, and gather whatever files or tools you need to be productive in the next 24 hours, including passwords to systems you need to access, driving directions to any appointments you have to drive to, phone numbers of people you need to call, and so forth.

It might take more than 20 minutes the first day, but over time you will get better at it and the investment will pay for itself in terms of peace of mind and increased productivity.

If you want more suggestions, and you are willing to invest a bit more time, I would suggest David Allen's Getting Things Done (https://goo.gl/r1Rvln) (a book and a methodology).

It is possible to be both tactical and strategic in the course of the day if you are organized and you build in time for planning. Try it and let me know how it goes.

All the best,

The Proposal Doctor

Ask the Proposal Doctor

Pounded by pricing?

Dear Proposal Doctor,

Please help. I am mid-way through a large and important government bid. The two or three people who have all the knowledge we need to document the solution are in pricing meetings that go on for hours, and by the time they start working on the non-price aspects of the proposal, they are exhausted and not productive.

I'm worried that we are going to miss interim deadlines and have to rush through our reviews and document production cycles. I don't know what to do because the pricing activity is like a "black box" to those of us who are not involved.

How can I change the priorities of these key people?

–Pounded by Pricing

Dear Pounded,

Actually, it might be your priorities that need to change. Although proposal managers have often steered clear of pricing, it is an essential element of the proposal and one that is often not efficiently managed. If you got engaged with pricing, you could probably rationalize the process and speed things up.

But there are other, more compelling reasons for you to start paying close attention to this activity. Decisions being made in those pricing meetings are certain to affect the rest of the proposal, and the sooner you know what those decisions are, the better. Likewise, the people engaged in pricing need to know what is going on in the other areas of the proposal, particularly anything that involves purchases of equipment, assignment or hiring of people, and real estate and facilities needed to meet RFP requirements.

Although some pricing models are detailed and technical, many are easy to understand. If you don't understand what is going on, ask someone to explain. This will let you make a judgment as to whether the long meetings are really necessary or simply an attractive alternative to writing proposal text.

Ultimately, you can't be responsible for the proposal document if you are not engaged in all facets of it—there are too many interdependencies.

So step up, and even if you can't speed the process up, you are likely to gain valuable knowledge and skills.

All the best,

The Proposal Doctor

Ask the Proposal Doctor

Stepping on toes?

Dear Proposal Doctor,

Despite a kick off meeting at which we discussed roles and responsibilities, everyone on this proposal seems to be stepping on everyone's toes. The coordinator keeps trying to do my job; the capture manager is trying to be the solution architect; the contracts representative is getting way too involved in pricing. We have redundancy and re-work in some areas and complete neglect in others. How can I get things back on track?

–Proposal-Manager-in-Chaos

Dear Proposal Manager,

I feel your pain and have lived through similar experiences. The root cause is an unwillingness to have a discussion of roles and responsibilities at the level of detail required. To emphasize those last six words: at the level of detail required. It is much easier to define roles in general terms.

Here is my favorite: *Responsible for red team.* What exactly does that mean? Does the responsible person find the room, order food, send invitations, print proposals, set up the room, dial the speaker phone, give instructions to evaluators, adjudicate all red team comments, facilitate the meeting, choose reviewers, schedule the review…? Unless you have a discussion that nails down these details, there will be confusion and overlap.

Here is one technique that might help: for each role, make sure the responsibilities are defined as concrete actions. "Plan red team" is not a concrete action because there is not a result. I won't know what it looks like when I am done. "Create list of reviewers," on the other hand, is a concrete action. Either I have the list or I don't.

Warning: these discussions are not fun. Typically, they are boring and can also be contentious. If, for example, the proposal coordinator feels stuck in an administrative role, drilling down on the details of that role will only reinforce those feelings. But, the payoff is huge because even if people don't like their list of responsibilities, at least they know what they are.

Try it on your next proposal and see what happens.

All the best,

The Proposal Doctor

Ask the Proposal Doctor

How to write technical volumes more efficiently?

Dear Proposal Doctor,

I work for a small business, and all our engineers work on a customer site while our business development/proposal staff work at our office (which is in another state). This makes writing the technical volume really difficult because we can't get our engineers on site to write. We end up having to travel a lot, which disrupts the proposal and takes people away from their families for weeks at a time. How could we write technical volumes more efficiently?

–Running Out of Ideas

Dear Running,

This is a situation many proposal managers face frequently, so I'm glad you wrote to me about it. In one respect, you are fortunate. You said you can't get your engineers to write. This is actually a good thing. Typically, engineers struggle with proposal writing. So, it's a great idea to team them up with someone who is an experienced writer. Professional writers know how to interview and draw the information out of subject matter experts (SME).

Working across locations is always a challenge, and it's difficult to give specific advice without knowing the average page count, content, and duration of your proposals. However, a proposal should have one location that is the center of gravity, and participants who can't be there should be required to use whatever tools are available to connect (Skype, collaborative tools, etc.).

So, the question for you is where should that center of gravity be? It sounds as though it should be where the company's office is. This will save wear and tear on staff, and it will save time and money.

What is the business development staff doing when they travel? Are they interviewing the engineers? Are they trying to manage the proposal from a customer site or a hotel room? Once you determine a center of gravity, you can break down the tasks and work on ways each can be accomplished from the home base. Maybe the team could conduct interviews using a webcam and digital tape recorder. Don't forget the camera—otherwise people will be multi-tasking and not giving the interview the attention it deserves.

Remote participation demands much more discipline and structure than are required when the team is collocated. Could the traveling be restricted to the early proposal stage when you are gathering information? These are just a few ideas, and you will probably have to experiment and refine until you come up with a process that works for your organization.

Have courage,

The Proposal Doctor

Ask the Proposal Doctor

Stop the madness?

Dear Proposal Doctor,

The company I work for is bidding on a large government contract, and the proposal is a huge undertaking. My team consists of more than 50 people, and my MS Project schedule has hundreds of lines. It's a challenge, which is to be expected. I was excited and optimistic when we started, but now I have a boatload of senior executives breathing down my neck. All the time! I spend at least half of every day explaining and justifying what we are doing to some vice president or other and the other half of the day managing the proposal. How can I get these people off my back?

–Pounded by Management

Dear Pounded,

Your frustration is understandable, and so is the behavior of your managers. The company is spending a lot on this proposal—in real cost as well as opportunity cost—if your team has 50 people on it. It is only natural that the executives in charge would want to understand your progress on a regular basis. If I were in your shoes, I would corral all the vice presidents and other Lord High Pooh Bahs whom you consider stakeholders, and set up a meeting to discuss proposal metrics and schedules.

The purpose of the meeting would be to agree on three items:

1. What metrics should be reported?
2. How frequently should they be reported?
3. What is the best format for the report?

Just as a good litigator never asks a question of the witness without already knowing the answer, I would have my own answer to each of these questions prepared in advance in order to steer the conversation towards those metrics and schedules that put the least strain on me and my team. Metrics I have used in similar situations include number of sections ready for pink team, number of pages written, number of graphics completed, and number of requirements addressed.

I have sometimes posted this information to a collaborative site and in other instances used a chart on butcher paper in the war room. When managing one very challenging proposal, I sent a voicemail to key stakeholders at 7:00 a.m. every day summarizing the previous day's activities.

These are just suggestions. Pick what works in your situation. Whatever you do, don't treat management as the enemy. An *us-versus-them* environment unites the team in the short term, but wears away at productivity after the initial thrill of battle. Moreover, your managers have a legitimate need for the information they are seeking. And finally, you might need their help at some point.

I am sure there is a way to give them the information they need in less than half your working day.

All the best,

The Proposal Doctor

Ask the Proposal Doctor

Stick to your knitting?

Dear Proposal Doctor,

We are a little more than halfway through the response time for a big, must-win bid. Red team madness is approaching. Big gaps exist. We have not road-tested the solution, and we are still missing resumes for people badly needed for us to be credible for this job. Two partners have yet to sign their teaming agreements. Yet the capture manager and the two senior executives with a lot to lose (or gain) are focused (read obsessed) with tiny proposal details such as the colors of the text boxes and the size of the fourth-level heading. How can I get these people to focus on the important things and let me do my job? Why would they want to do my job? I can't understand this!

–Confused and Bewildered

Dear Confused,

This problem is so common that it is almost a pathology unto itself. Here is the simple fact: people do what they know how to do. I once found a manager of a 2,000-page volume, under incredible time pressure, measuring the space between the bullets. Senior executives don't really want to be desktop publishers—but it is much easier to appear competent at that than to appear incompetent at addressing the big problems. And it is always possible, although probably unlikely, that they don't really have confidence in your abilities. Either way, their behavior is destructive. It threatens the viability of the proposal document, and it undermines your credibility, even though that is probably not their intent.

I don't know whether or not you had a discussion of roles and responsibilities at the outset of the proposal. If you did, and if those roles were documented, you can use the definitions to remind your capture manager and executives that specialization is a good thing. Desktop publishers have their expertise, and so do capture managers. It's a waste of resources for us to do each other's jobs.

If you did not have this conversation, or if you had it but didn't document it, you need to arrange a meeting with these micro-managers now. This is a conversation that would be good to rehearse with a friend or colleague before the actual event. Try to ascertain whether or not the capture manager and executives have a reason to doubt your abilities. If they don't, then it will be much easier to point out the folly of more than one person performing the identical function. It would help to have a neutral party present—someone respected by all who understands the position you are in and the danger to the proposal effort. Doing what is right for the proposal needs to be the focal point, not whether or not someone is doing his or her job. If the capture manager can't get the partners to sign the teaming agreements, who can? Document the results of the meeting to remind participants of the agreements you reach.

Going forward, articulate roles at the beginning in a very concrete way. It's tempting to skip this step or to define roles at a high level. It isn't pleasant or interesting to spell out every proposal function and get agreement about who will perform it. Yet the more general the discussion, the more room for misinterpretation and frustration down the road.

You still have time to get this situation back on track—please use it wisely.

All the best,

The Proposal Doctor

Ask the Proposal Doctor

Waiting by the phone?

Dear Proposal Doctor,

One subject matter expert (SME) in my company has the bulk of the information we need for the technical proposal. It is all in his head. This person is very busy with clients all day and keeps telling me that he will write the sections assigned to him at night—and that he will meet the deadline. We are a week into the writing period, and so far, he has produced nothing. He is inaccessible all day and often does not answer his cell phone in the evening. I have left messages every day for the past week— sometimes several a night—but he has not called back. Panic is setting in. Please help!

–Waiting by the Phone

Dear Waiting,

First, let's face facts. This SME is not going to call you. So don't bother waiting by the phone. Now, let's go to the underlying assumption in your letter, which is that you cannot get the proposal done without this guy. Can someone validate that? Is this person really so brilliant and indispensable? Says who? Has this person written proposals before? Can anyone show you what he wrote? It might be that he is not producing because he can't or doesn't know how.

If it turns out that he is not the only person in the universe who can write this section, you will probably have an easy out, since your SME will likely be happy to be let off the hook. Get rid of him, or change his role and ask him to be a reviewer. If your SME is, in fact, the only person who can do the work, you have no choice but to escalate. I know this guy is important and so very busy, but he is not, after all, President of the United States. He reports to someone. There is a manager or supervisor above him. That is the person whom you should be calling—not to complain, but simply to express concern that the SME is out of touch.

Then, get real. It is a truly rare professional who can deal effectively with clients all day and churn out beautiful proposal prose for several hours in the evening—in fact if you know such a person, please send me his or her contact information. I have never met one!

So consider another way of interacting with your SME. Set up a time to talk to your SME every evening and interview him to get the information you need, or have an experienced proposal writer conduct the interviews. Either way, I strongly recommend taping the conversations. There are a lot of people who are much better at explaining something verbally than they are at writing it down.

I also have some advice for you on your next proposal. It sounds as though this person did not have a clear understanding of your expectations in the first place, and you appear to have waited and hoped for the best for an entire week. Hope is not a method. Think about that once you get through your current crisis, which I know you will, once you see the situation for what it is.

All the best,

The Proposal Doctor

Ask the Proposal Doctor

The big chance?

Dear Proposal Doctor,

You must help. The senior proposal manager has gone on emergency medical leave, and the big and long-anticipated RFP is in my lap. This is hugely scary for me. I have never managed something this big and complex. So much is riding on a winning response—my heart is racing, and I am escalating into panic mode as I type these words. Should I just tell management that I am not up to the job? What to do?

–Worried and Panicked

Dear Worried,

Only you can make the determination as to whether or not to throw in the towel. If you do, it will be hard for your management to promote you or assign you to increasingly challenging proposals in the future. You will have taken yourself out of the running for advancement. So, unless you have a personal situation that precludes your taking on the assignment, I encourage you to go for it.

If you are a runner, you know that most runners can actually run twice as long as their longest run. So, often people training for a 10k never run more than 5k. They do just fine on race day. The same applies to proposals—you can probably manage a proposal twice as hard as the hardest one you have managed to date.

My advice comes with two caveats—if you can't do these two things, you should tell your management to find someone else. First, get a mentor who will be willing to talk to you and guide you through this experience—every day if necessary. If you don't know of someone, go through the discussions on LinkedIn that relate to proposal management and see if you can identify someone whose opinion you trust and respect. You would be surprised how many people are willing to help someone in a situation like yours.

Second, never let the team see you sweat. When you are with your proposal team, you must exude confidence, even if you don't feel it. Strong leadership will unite the team behind you, and they will support you if they are convinced they can win—and they will be convinced if you are convinced.

Do whatever you have to do behind the scenes to reduce anxiety. If you can manage those two things, this will be an excellent growth experience and one that might not come along again. Welcome it and jump in. I am sure you can swim, and you will soon be advising others to do the same.

All the best,

The Proposal Doctor

Ask the Proposal Doctor

Two hats?

Dear Proposal Doctor,

People say I have a big head, but believe me, I would prefer to only wear one hat. Unfortunately, my capture manager is not doing his job. Communications with subcontractors are erratic and inconsistent, the pricing team does not have a strategy, and progress towards a viable solution is slow. Every time I jump in to help with these items, the team is so grateful to have someone providing direction. In fact, if not for my efforts, nothing would have been accomplished on many fronts that should be the responsibility of the capture manager. Wearing two hats is exhausting and I'm only getting compensated for one. How can I get my capture manager to do his job?

–Double Hatted

Dear Double,

The situation you describe is common in two respects. First, it is common to find many different definitions of capture. This job is not in the Standard Occupational Classification System.

Your capture manager probably thinks he is doing his job. To make it clear what is expected of him, you and he need to have a conversation about roles and responsibilities at a very concrete level ("Determine target rates for subcontractors and communicate those rates 1 week after RFP release"). It's always easier to avoid these detailed discussions, but at one's peril.

Second, this is common because so many proposal managers develop the *workaround* syndrome. This is a term from organizational behavior studies that examined the way in which employees find a workaround for a problem rather than dealing with the underlying cause. Nurses in hospitals have been known to pay (with their own money) for taxis to deliver laundry when the hospital linen service did not deliver clean sheets on time. It gets the bed changed, but does nothing for the next nurse who needs clean linens. If you continue to wear two hats, your capture manager will never learn what is expected of him. You owe it to him, yourself, and the organization to address this head-on. Now.

This will not be an easy conversation, so prepare for it, and maybe even rehearse your part out loud, or with a trusted colleague.

All the best,

The Proposal Doctor

Ask the Proposal Doctor

How to build professional skills in proposal management?

Dear Proposal Doctor,

I have been in proposals for five years and love the industry. I am one of those anomalies that thrive on little sleep, junk food, and a drive to win! I am hungry to improve and learn as much as I can.

Besides joining the Association of Proposal Management Professionals (APMP), what else do you suggest I do to improve my skills, knowledge, and general competency in proposal management?

–The "Green" Proposal Manager"

Dear Green,

Great question. I admire your commitment to continuous improvement.

Knowledge is experiential in this business. At the same time, proposal managers need skills that are inherent in other professions.

First, consider courses or online training that will improve communication skills, both written and spoken. For written communication, look at courses offered in technical writing in a local community college, through the Society for Technical Communication, or online. Many organizations offer training in public speaking, and Toastmasters is an excellent, inexpensive way to improve those skills and gain confidence as well.

Second, make sure you are proficient in the main desktop applications. This is important not because proposal managers should always do their own desktop publishing (arguably, they shouldn't), but because they need to understand the tools used by the production team. This helps in estimating the proposal budget and in creating realistic deadlines. Lynda.com offers excellent courses on MS Office and Adobe applications, just to name two.

Third, leadership development is critical for proposal managers. A good leadership development program will include a 360° (or equivalent) review and the chance to see yourself as others see you through video and other tools. The local community college might offer courses in organizational development, and the major online universities do as well—University of Phoenix, Walden University, and Capella University. Don't laugh. These schools are accredited and, thanks to the Internet, the quality is kept high. Do some homework before enrolling in a formal degree program, as these can be expensive. Professional societies such as the American Management Association and Women in Technology also offer leadership development programs. Again, do the research. Quality varies.

Finally, I think that all proposal managers would benefit from having been in a sales or business development position, and if you haven't, I recommend sales training. We are so dependent on business development and sales professionals, so it is very important to understand their mindset.

Happy learning!

The Proposal Doctor

Ask the Proposal Doctor

Capture manager creates chaos in post-RFP collaboration?

Dear Proposal Doctor,

Please help me to not kill my capture manager! This person is still running some of the meetings even though the RFP is out. The meetings are long and rambling. There are no agendas and no action items.

Proposal contributors are losing faith that we know what we are doing. They want to work on their sections. I am afraid that the energy is sapping out of the team just at the time that it should be ramping up.

Since my jurisdiction has concealed hand-gun laws, although I would like to resort to violence, I need some alternatives in dealing with this situation.

–Ready to Kill

Dear Ready,

Yikes! It is hard to change course once a syndrome like this sets in. But it can be done.

First, you need to have a heart-to-heart with the capture manager to explain that since time is now of the essence, with the RFP out, it is important for contributors to meet their deadlines.

Second, suggest a standard format for all meetings —your capture manager's as well as yours and everyone else's–that includes a formal invitation, an agenda, a time limit, and defined out puts and action items. When time is precious, this is only good sense and good management. It should be received as a reasonable request. I would think about escalating if you and the capture manager cannot come to a satisfactory agreement.

Having said this, it is important to remember that if the team is still working through the solution, consensus and shared understanding are important. There are times, and meetings, when everyone's voice has to be heard to avoid confusion (and dissent) down the road. It is often painful, but the alternative is worse. That is a judgment call, meeting by meeting, and although you might not always agree with the capture manager's decision, you should respect it. (Within limits.)

Sincerely,

The Proposal Doctor

Ask the Proposal Doctor

Creating an optimal path for a losing proposal?

Dear Proposal Doctor:

I am currently the proposal manager on what I believe to be a losing proposal. We have never met the customer and have no first-hand insight to the customer's requirements or hot buttons. Our technical architect has developed a solution that meets 75% of the customer's requirements. My management is very enthusiastic about our chances of winning. What should I do?

Sincerely,

–Troubled

Dear Troubled,

As proposal managers, we have to develop a range of skills and behaviors. Right now, your job is to learn to compartmentalize (not easy) so that you can take three steps:

1. State your position.
2. Get on with the show, because the show must go on.
3. Address the long term.

Here is what I mean.

First, if you have not already informed senior management that this should be a no-bid, you should state all the reasons why the company is probably wasting its money on this bid. Be clear, concise, and factual. Leave out the emotional dimension. Then put it behind you.

The second step is playing the hand you were dealt. Put your concerns aside and do the best you can, given the constraints of your situation. Actually, we all do this all the time, because every proposal has some kind of ridiculous constraint—it could be a page count, an inconsistent RFP, whatever. Our job is to live (and sometimes excel) within those constraints. So you really do have to forget about the first step once it is done.

Third, when this mess is over, you need to address the long term. Do you want to continue to work in an environment where you only do pop-up proposals? There are employers and clients who qualify deals and who know the customer. Be warned, however, that those tend to be the larger companies. Large companies come with their own baggage (internal reviews, burdensome processes). Life is about tradeoffs.

I hope this helps. Meanwhile, as the French say, *courage*!

The Proposal Doctor

Ask the Proposal Doctor

Faking deadlines foils confidence in proposal team?

Dear Proposal Doctor,

How can I get my clients to communicate the schedule accurately? We provide print and graphic services, so we are just one part of the proposal machine. Often the clients don't communicate about extensions and leave us waiting for information. Or they give fake deadlines. I believe their intent is to get the product back faster or instill a greater sense of urgency. What actually happens is chaos, which prevents accurate scheduling.

My staff cannot prioritize without accurate deadlines for multiple projects. Even worse, there is a loss of trust. If the vendor isn't given timely or accurate information, it communicates that the person with the information doesn't trust enough or respect their resource enough to share it. That makes it harder to work together in an open environment after that.

–Frustrated and Indignant

Dear Frustrated,

Wow! You raise some important issues. Let's take the fake deadlines first. In fact, every proposal manager is tempted to pad the schedule and ask for things earlier than they are needed. My own belief is that this is acceptable only to a degree, and only if it is explained. I always put extra days in the schedule for production, because you never know when someone is going to have a sick child, a car crash, a weather-related crisis, or some other personal emergency. I explain this to the team, and I keep the padding to a realistic minimum. I usually have historical examples I can cite that validate my assumptions.

Padding the schedule for any other reason communicates the proposal manager's lack of confidence in the work ethic of the team, the quality of work that will be produced, or both. If there is no confidence, it's time to swap out the team and get new people. People will work to the standards that are communicated. Low expectations will result in low quality. People who engage in this behavior are convinced that they are out-smarting the system and it might be difficult to get them to adopt another approach. But it is worth trying. If they don't understand or won't change, you need to move on.

As to not communicating the schedule, I suggest you address this at the outset of your next job. This has to be one of the rules of engagement, and it needs to be clearly articulated. You need to tell your clients what you expect of them. Put it in writing if you have to, and then hold them accountable. Live by the sword; die by the sword! If they can't live up to it, they are not desirable clients and you need to devote some business development time to finding better ones. It will pay off in the long run.

All the best,

The Proposal Doctor

Professional Improvement

Six lessons learned from an industry conference

Lisa Pafe

I recently returned from an Association of Proposal Management Professionals (APMP) Bid & Proposal Con. Networking with more than 800 business development, capture, and proposal professionals from around the world was both exhilarating and exhausting. I want to share some lessons learned on how to best leverage the opportunities available over 4 days of workshops, panels, presentations, vendor booth promos, receptions, dinners, and more.

Be all there. As an attendee and presenter, I noticed those ever-present smart phones are quite a distraction. Make a concerted effort to be present wherever you are. If the presentation is not of interest to you, then go ahead and leave rather than staring at your phone and disrespecting the presenter. If you are sharing a table at lunch, join in the conversation rather than checking your email.

Execute your message. You should attend a conference with the goal of executing your message. For example, if you want to find mentors, then make sure people learn that fact when they speak to you. If you want to promote your expertise in a specific topic, whether or not you are a presenter, you can participate in interactive sessions, add to relevant conversations, and contribute to social media. By the time you leave the conference, you should also leave the desired impression with your colleagues.

Don't sit next to your friends. It is quite tempting to stay within your comfort zone. However, if you sit next to someone you don't know and/or want to know better, the networking will result in a new contact that may be valuable now or in the future.

Take time to enjoy the venue. Leave the hotel. Get out and see the sights because playing tourist is part of the total experience. Share sightseeing with others to increase networking value and build relationships.

Analyze the return on investment (ROI). The benefits of attending a conference are both quantifiable and non-quantifiable, but the costs are real. Costs include time spent preparing for the conference, opportunity costs of time lost, as well as the more obvious costs such as travel, lodging, food, and registration. Free conference ROI calculators are a big help in understanding costs and benefits.

Follow up. Do not neglect the follow up. You gathered a lot of business cards and attended useful presentations. Reach out to new and existing contacts after the conference to keep the conversation going, thus continuing to execute your message and achieve better ROI.

5 rules of worrying

Lisa Pafe

The Buddhist rule on worrying (https://goo.gl/IghQYH) is simple: if you can create change, do it. If you cannot change a situation, stop worrying about it. Worrying about things you cannot change increases stress and reduces productivity.

This rule is very applicable to our personal and business aspirations. But how do we know which situations are ripe for change and are therefore worth our worry? Follow these five golden rules of when to worry.

1. You can solve the problem. Examine the situation as objectively as possible. Make a list of action items you can accomplish or assign to others in order to solve the problem or at least contribute to the solution. If there are none, then move on.

2. You can influence the decision. We are often faced with having to accept a decision we do not like. Either we have stated our opinion and it has been rejected by the decision-maker, or we have no voice in the decision. If you cannot influence the decision, you have no choice but to focus your attention and your worry elsewhere.

3. You can stop wasting time. We often feel pressed for time, juggling our multitude of business and personal responsibilities with imperfect success, leading to more and more worry and anxiety. Take the time to examine your schedule. Time management apps (https://goo.gl/bjicbB) that you can download to your smartphone, laptop, or tablet abound. Free and paid versions include features such as the ability to define and time personal and work activities, review time logs and calendars, run detailed reports and pie charts, back up data, and export results to fully analyze how you spend your time and thus gain greater productivity. Greater productivity reduces worry.

4. You can correct misinformation. Often the very problems we seek to solve, the decisions we seek to influence, and the time we seek to manage are adversely impacted by misinformation. Of course, we often see the facts misrepresented or spun to favor our opponents. Despite this obstacle, we do have the responsibility to present correct information to the best of our ability. Once you have presented the facts as you know them, they may help solve the problem, influence the decision, or remove time wasters, but if they don't, your worry is only wasting your energy and time.

5. You can improve. You should worry about improving yourself because personal growth is totally under your control. If you have tried your best, then stop worrying. Your best may be imperfect, but if it is the best you can do today, it is perfect for you.

It is human to worry, and our angst often drives us to greater success. By focusing on these five productive areas of worry, we can reduce unnecessary stress and improve productivity.

The benefits of understanding dissenting perspectives

Build credibility you can wield to resolve conflict, muscle through roadblocks, and challenge teams to higher standards

Julia Quigley

In the business world, it's easy to rush our decisions and our conversations. How often have you been in meetings when people speak over one other, cutting in as ideas come to them? That level of intensity and quick thinking has benefits, but it can also lead to people only expressing their own thoughts instead of really understanding other perspectives in the room.

Seth Godin advises us to identify the generous skeptics in our workplaces (https://goo.gl/8xRijt)—those people offering an opinion who have insight into our field or into our personal performance—and listen to them instead of dismissing them. As we understand these other perspectives more completely, we build a rapport with the generous critics, and we make our own ideas more robust. There really isn't a downside, because as Godin points out, we always have time to ignore them later.

The benefits of listening and understanding our colleagues' perspectives aren't limited to those identified above; when we take the time to pause and engage dissenting opinions, we have increased credibility in the office that we can use to diffuse conflict, muscle through proposal roadblocks, and challenge our proposal teams to achieve more.

To illustrate, a frustrated business developer recently wrote to *Washington BizJournals* asking how to resolve an ongoing conflict with a colleague whose refusal to collaborate was sabotaging the business developer's output. Advice columnist Alice Waagen explains that understanding is the keystone for resolution (https://goo.gl/BwFnwI). By focusing on understanding the cause of a conflict instead of expressing our own frustrations, we can create a solution instead of a power struggle.

In addition to resolving conflicts, when we store up credibility with our colleagues by understanding their perspectives, we can strategically blow through those stores to get through roadblocks in the way of a proposal's success. Rachel Salaman describes recent work by German psychologists who advocate using our darker emotions to our benefit in the office (https://goo.gl/QGYrFI); one of their assertions is that if we have a reputation as an understanding and interested person, people are more likely to take us seriously when we object to someone working outside of the proposal process or imposing impossible requirements.

And finally, when we've built credibility through listening and understanding, we can challenge our teams to new heights. Karen Hurt writes about why we resist high achievement (https://goo.gl/X4bimK)—harder work and personal sacrifice—as well as the benefits—quality work products, self-confidence, extrinsic rewards, and team bonding. Despite a team's resistance, if we have a history of listening to dissenters and understanding alternate perspectives, our proposal teams will be more inclined to trust our leadership.

As you enter your meetings this week, consider slowing the pace of the discussions or circling back with colleagues off-line to discuss dissenting opinions; you can always ignore them later, and in the meantime you'll be building credibility you can wield to resolve conflict, muscle through roadblocks, and challenge them to higher standards.

Give your brain space to work

Julia Quigley

Life around the beltway seems to move faster than life in the rest of the United States. Add in managing proposals, and not only is it impossible to cross off each item on your to-do list, taking a minute to clear your head feels inconceivable. In contrast with the frenetic pace of federal proposals, our work products are better if we can delay some tasks to give our brains room to think.

In his blog post "Take Time to Not Think," Scott Eblin shares that our best problem-solving happens during a mixture of conscious and unconscious thought (https://goo.gl/OBdj6Z). This is the type of thinking we have when we're in the shower or waiting in a long line. Because our brains continue to work through issues "in the background," we find ourselves chewing on work problems or finding inspiration when we give our minds time to wander.

The busier our personal and professional lives are, the harder it is to imagine finding that time for ourselves, so consider the following list of suggestions taken from Eblin's blog along with some of our own ideas:

- Turn off the radio or podcasts during your commute, work around the house, or exercise routine.
- Take a break from your workday to walk around the building.
- Eat lunch on your own, away from your computer and phone.
- Set aside a few minutes to meditate or take an uninterrupted coffee break during the slowest part of your day.

Another way to give your brain extra time to process is what Ruth Hill calls *active procrastination*. Her approach is to do the prep work for a task and then set it aside while she works on other more immediate tasks. Delaying the task gives her brain extra time to process the prep work, giving her a clearer perspective about what needs to be done when she comes back to the task.

To illustrate this concept in federal proposals, consider the following example. After an RFP is released, you might be conflicted about how to outline the proposal given some unclear RFP instructions. Rather than spinning your wheels, set that task aside until later in the day. In the meantime, work on your kickoff slides, adapt your proposal template, or work on another proposal for a bit. When you come back to the outlining task, your brain will be better prepared for the challenge than it was earlier. If you're lucky, the government may have even released an RFP revision.

Whether you're consciously giving your brain the opportunity to wander or asking it to continue working out a puzzle in the background, the practice of delaying select tasks can improve your productivity and creativity.

Proposal yoga

Yoga has multiple aspects beneficial to capture and proposal professionals

Lisa Pafe

Yoga has several aspects that are beneficial to capture and proposal professionals. These include breathing, mindfulness, meditation, and the poses themselves.

Breathing. Did you know that yoga is more about breathing than about poses? Stress and hurrying (everyday hazards of our profession!) cause us to breathe shallowly and too quickly. Every cell in the body requires oxygen, and our level of vitality is a product of the health of our cells. Shallow breathing does not exercise the lungs sufficiently, so they lose some of their function, causing a further reduction in vitality and productivity.

Mindfulness. The practice of mindfulness can help you focus your brain and accomplish more that matters. Mindfulness is about awareness. It also involves acceptance. Try to pay attention to your thoughts and feelings without judging them.

Focus on the task at hand without rehashing the past or worrying about the future.

Meditation. Meditation relaxes the mind and body. A simple meditation to do at your desk is a breathing meditation, during which you focus on your breath, thus practicing mindfulness. This will calm your mind and relax your body.

Begin by finding a comfortable position, but one in which you will not fall asleep. Sitting with your hands resting lightly in your lap is a good position to try. Or, gently touch thumb and forefinger together.

Roll your shoulders slowly forward and then slowly back. Lean your head from side to side, slowly and carefully lowering your left ear toward your left shoulder, and then your right ear toward your right shoulder.

Focus inward on your third eye (between your eyebrows). Set your intention for the day ahead. Set it as a positive affirmation. For example, if you want to be productive, think *I am productive*. If you want to relax, think *I am relaxing*.

Relax all your muscles. Unclench your jaw and your brow. Observe your breathing. Notice how your breath flows in and out. At first, make no effort to change your breathing in any way, simply notice how your body breathes. Sit quietly, seeing in your mind's eye your breath flowing gently in and out of your body.

When your attention wanders, as it will, just focus back again on your breathing. If you can't focus easily, you can think to yourself, I breathe in…I breathe out…

Notice the stages of a complete breath…from the in breath…to the pause that follows…the exhale…and the pause before taking another breath…

Enjoy the slight breaks between each breath.

As thoughts intrude, allow them to pass, and return your attention to your breathing.

Feel your chest and stomach gently rise and fall with each breath.

Now, as you inhale, count silently…one, two, three.

Hold for a moment.

As you exhale, count…one, two, three.

Hold for a moment, and now let's repeat two more times.

Inhale…one, two, three.

Exhale…one, two, three.

Inhale…one, two, three.

Exhale…one, two, three.

Notice now how your body feels. Gently open your eyes if they are closed. Feel rejuvenated.

Proposal Yoga. I have written and presented extensively on the benefits of proposal yoga. Try this detoxifying spinal twist:

- Sit in your chair, cross one leg over the other, and grasp your top knee with your opposite hand.
- Hold the back of your chair with your free hand and slowly twist your upper body and head towards that arm, keeping your back and neck as straight as possible. Hold for 10 counts.
- Switch your legs and arms and twist in the opposite direction.

You can access my article with additional proposal yoga poses here (https://goo.gl/NISBm7) and one of my presentations on proposal yoga here (https://goo.gl/hV9vor). Learn how to reduce stress, increase flexibility, and regain composure—at your desk. Namaste!

Dealing with employment dissatisfaction: change what's in your control

When faced with workplace dissatisfaction, most people try to change their environments when they should be changing themselves

Julia Quigley

Few of us have ever worked in an ideal proposal shop. In most casual conversations at conferences and social gatherings, proposal professionals reveal exasperation with some aspect of their company—a disconnect between upper management and proposal managers, lack of resources, or long hours. Employees who are unsatisfied at work often try to change their workplace, which is a futile exercise. Unless an employee is in a position of power, it's unlikely he or she can solve the larger issues leading to dissatisfaction.

To get a reprieve at work, it's more useful to examine what changes you can make to your own behaviors and beliefs.

If you're frustrated by the amount of hours you're working and feeling trapped, read Michael Hyatt's post about identifying and breaking through your own limiting beliefs (https://goo.gl/h4UW9g). According to Hyatt, you could be underestimating your own agency, falsely believing there are no other options, or you could be too drained to pursue alternatives and develop a plan. If you decide the best option is to stay in your current position, identify coping techniques that work for you.

For example, we all need to take breaks, so be strategic about your breaks. Stay away from Facebook or idle chit-chat. Instead, you could take up Lisa Pafe's Proposal Yoga (https://goo.gl/FwCr5B) practice to ease tension during the work day, or you could eat lunch away from your desk and take an afternoon stroll—two of the top takeaways from our post about boosting creativity (https://goo.gl/3tHGIO) . In addition to strategies to help your overall tension, identify ways to cope with specific stresses in your environment.

If your workplace strife stems from a disconnect in proposal ideology between key players, you should examine your own beliefs with as much scrutiny as your opposition might. In his recent blog post, "Superstitions at Work," (https://goo.gl/eYUXBd) Seth Godin explores how we often hold on to beliefs that aren't factual because they're comfortable or make us feel like we're in control. We often succumb to confirmation bias, interpreting evidence in favor of our conclusions and disregarding experiences that complicate those beliefs.

To see if your position is supported, review relevant data and materials from industry resources, such as the APMP Body of Knowledge (https://goo.gl/19y45r). If your organization hasn't been collecting relevant metrics, begin the process and assess the resulting data at a future time. If you still hold your original opinions after the review, you'll be prepared for a fact-based (rather than feeling-based) discussion with your colleagues. If you change opinion after the review, you'll be prepared to start a new conversation with your coworkers.

Whatever challenges you're facing, the goal is to identify what you can change about your own behaviors and thoughts, even if the problematic situation stems from other people.

This is a difficult mental practice made easier by discussions with your peers. Start participating in your local APMP chapter meetings or attend conferences so you can hear how others are managing similar challenges. You'll come away inspired with new ideas of what you can do to improve in a dissatisfying situation.

Calming your monkey mind

Lisa Pafe

We are all frantically busy. We can't relax. Our down time is spent checking Twitter, Instagram, Facebook, etc. Our minds are twisting, swinging in all directions, and leaping from branch to branch.

In Buddhism it is aptly called *Monkey Mind*. And it impacts your health by increasing stress as well as your productivity by reducing your ability to focus.

Take 5 minutes to calm your mind, and I guarantee you will have a calmer and more productive day. Try this simple breathing and meditation exercise.

Close your eyes or focus gently on one spot in the room. Set your intention for the day ahead. Set it as a positive affirmation. For example, if you want to be calm today, think: "I am calm." If you want to be productive, think: "I am productive."

Now, roll your shoulders slowly forward and then slowly back. Lean your head gently from side to side, lowering your left ear toward your left shoulder, and then your right ear toward your right shoulder. Relax your muscles. Unclench your jaw, and relax the furrow in your brow.

Observe your breathing. Notice how your breath flows in and out. Don't change your breathing, but simply notice how your body breathes. Sit quietly, imagining your breath flowing gently in and out of your body.

When your attention wanders, as it will, just focus back again on your breathing. If you can't focus easily, think to yourself, "I breathe in…I breathe out…"

Notice any stray thoughts, but don't dwell on them. Simply let the thoughts pass.

See how your breath continues to flow…deeply… calmly. As thoughts intrude, allow them to pass, and return to your breathing. As you inhale, count silently…one, two, three. Hold for a moment. As you exhale, count…one, two, three. Hold for a moment, and repeat several times.

Notice now how your body feels. Keeping your eyes closed, register the sounds around you. Feel the floor beneath your feet. Feel your clothes against your body. Remember your positive affirmation for the day.

Wiggle your fingers and toes. Shrug your shoulders. Open your eyes, but remain sitting for a few moments longer. Then, straighten out your legs, and stretch your arms and legs gently.

Experience your body reawakening and your mind returning to the tasks at hand. Feel the increased energy for the tasks ahead. By calming your mind and body, you can clear your head to make way for maximum productivity! Namaste!

In search of new cheese – avoid stagnation

Maryann Lesnick

When I learned of the topic for a recent APMP-NCA eZine, one of my favorite books came to mind—Who Moved My Cheese? (https://goo.gl/ORKfNS) by Spencer Johnson, MD. The story is a metaphor about life. It's about dealing with change and avoiding stagnation. It's a parable that takes place in a maze. Four characters live in the maze, and they must search for "Cheese" to survive. The maze is long and confusing, and the Cheese is often difficult to find.

The characters include Sniff and Scurry, who are mice. They are non-analytical and non-judgmental. They just want Cheese and are willing to do whatever it takes to get it. The other two characters are Hem and Haw, mouse-size humans who have an entirely different relationship with Cheese. It's not just sustenance to them—it's their self-image, their belief system—and they become emotionally attached to the Cheese they have found.

The Cheese is a metaphor for the things we pursue in life—our jobs, careers, and relationships. The maze is how we navigate through the challenges we face in our pursuit of that Cheese.

As the four characters search for Cheese, the story reveals traits that either help them move forward or hold them back. It reveals how stagnation, apathy, complacency, entitlement, and blindness can affect the search for new Cheese.

One thing is certain, the Cheese is always changing and moving, and we need to change with it to survive. When the Cheese runs out, it's time to put on our running shoes and search for new Cheese.

Can you relate to these characters?

- **Sniff.** Who can smell change in the air; always on the lookout for opportunities; acts more than reacts; likes to keep options open.
- **Scurry.** Who goes into action immediately; not afraid to try new ideas; acts more than reacts; likes to keep things simple.

- **Hem.** Who does not want to change; afraid to take risks; overanalyzes situations; reacts more than acts; likes to stay in his comfort zone. "It's not fair!"
- **Haw.** Who is startled by change; likes to procrastinate; but then accepts change and moves on to enjoy New Cheese.

At different points in life, or even at different points of my day, I can be any of the four! During the story, Haw begins to write notes on the walls of the maze ("Writing on the Wall") that hold lessons for us. They reveal ways to turn our Hems into Haws. Here are some of the lessons we can learn from the book:

- Change your beliefs about change. See change not as a threat but an opportunity. Make it work to your advantage.
- The more you learn about the maze, the easier it will be to navigate.
- Imagine new Cheese. "Fake it until you make it." See yourself enjoying the new Cheese and make it a reality. Imagining yourself enjoying new Cheese will lead you to it.

- Why is it sometimes we cannot find new Cheese? The missing ingredient might be PASSION!
- Instead of falling behind and complaining about how inconvenient changes are, stay ahead of the game and learn new concepts. Take risks and don't be afraid.
- Many of us don't move until we feel comfortable and safe. But growth does not come from stagnation, it comes from change. Though difficult, if we embrace change, we will find new Cheese.
- As humans, we all resist change. We hide behind our fears, insecurities, lies, food, alcohol, toys, comfort zones, stubbornness, or whatever else keeps us stuck. But these are just delaying the inevitable.
- Change is inevitable. Monitor your environment and anticipate change. Your Cheese may disappear!
- Noticing small changes early helps you adapt to the bigger changes that are to come.
- The quicker you let go of old Cheese, the sooner you find new Cheese. New Cheese

is often better. Old beliefs do not lead you to new Cheese!

- When the Cheese moves, you either need to move with the Cheese or find new Cheese. Do not stay where there is no Cheese.
- It is safer to search the maze than remain in a Cheeseless situation.
- When you move beyond your fear, you will feel free.
- When you change what you believe, you change what you do.
- The fastest way to change is to laugh at your own folly—then you can let go and quickly move on.
- And finally, **nothing gets better until you change**.

Change comes in many ways, but two that stand out are those we initiate (proactive—a new job) and those that are imposed/forced on us (reactive—a layoff). In change, we find opportunities for growth—for finding new Cheese. As the writing on the wall states, "If You Do Not Change, You Can Become Extinct." We need to monitor, anticipate, adapt, and most importantly, enjoy change!

Capture and proposal innovations: heed the law of physics

Lisa Pafe

Newton's first law of motion states that "an object at rest tends to remain at rest, and an object in motion tends to remain in motion." Scientists call this tendency *inertia*.

The same holds true for our professional growth. When we do the same thing day after day, our aspirations wither on the vine. When you enable stagnation by remaining at rest, you end up making yourself and those around you miserable.

Are you stuck in your cubicle or war room staring at the four walls and wondering how to ignite fresh career growth? So many of us think that being a great capture or proposal professional involves a lot of time at the office. We tell ourselves that now isn't the right time to try something new, that we're too busy to find time to work out, much less explore new career avenues. Somehow, it's never the right time to leave our comfort zone.

So, like the law of physics with regard to inertia, we remain at rest. Luckily, so many opportunities are right in front of us to remain in motion.

Pursue APMP Certification

Either take the first step to get Foundation certified or the next to obtain Practitioner or even Professional level certification. Studies have shown that certification offers clear return on investment (ROI) through career progression and professional impact.

According to APMP, certification (https://goo.gl/5UyxiL) offers the following benefits:

1. Demonstrates you are serious about your career and profession.

2. Improves your own business development capabilities.

3. Provides an independent validation of your knowledge, skills, and leadership abilities.

4. Enhances how others in the organization see you and how you see yourself.

5. Defines and validates your role as a professional contributor.

Certification mentors are willing to help if you are uncertain how to proceed.

Participate in APMP at the International or Chapter Level

At the local level, APMP-NCA is largest Chapter in the United States with nearly 1,100 diverse business development, capture, and proposal professionals. Serving on the APMP-NCA Board or participating on one of the Board committees brings clear benefits:

1. Expands your network of peers, professional contacts, and community thought leaders.
2. Helps you develop and grow as a leader.
3. Cultivates new skills and experiences.
4. Makes an impact on the capture and proposal community.
5. Rounds out your own resume.

Contact any of us on the APMP-NCA Board of Directors (https://goo.gl/pI9fiL), and we will find the perfect opportunity for you to participate and grow professionally!

Be heard!

APMP-NCA (https://goo.gl/SZne1l) offers members the chance to present new ideas, share strategies, and start a dialogue with peers at quarterly Speaker Series events, live webinars, our annual Mid-Atlantic Conference & Expo, and our Capture Breakfast. You can also be heard by writing an *Executive Summary* eZine article or a blog post. Public speaking and professional writing opportunities help avoid stagnation with the following unbeatable benefits:

1. Provides a venue to meet new or strengthen existing contacts.
2. Improves communication skills.
3. Shares your ideas with the professional community.
4. Rounds out your resume.
5. Boosts self-esteem.

Join APMP-NCA's Mentor-Protégé Program

This award winning program invites the industry's best and brightest to partner together for professional growth.

Our program:

1. Builds lasting professional and personal relationships.
2. Bridges the generation gap.
3. Shares lessons learned.
4. Helps you learn about the Chapter and our members.
5. Adds yet another item to your resume.

With all of these great professional growth opportunities, it is hard to imagine how any of our members could fall prey to inertia!

From the experts: favorite business books to start the year

Business development, capture and proposal management, and leadership gurus share their must reads

Beth Wingate

At the end of last year, I asked a number of my favorite business development, capture and proposal management, and leadership gurus for their recommendations of *must-read* and *all-time favorite* business books.

Everyone generously provided a plethora of suggestions—many of which have taken up residence on my iPad or added to my UPS driver's many deliveries!

Here are their suggestions so you can learn more and hopefully find some new favorites. Please feel free to send your own suggestions to me at BWingate@LohfeldConsulting.com to share with everyone in a future post.

- *The 7 Habits of Highly Effective People: Powerful Lessons in Personal Change* by Stephen Covey (recommended by Mike Parkinson).
- A really good dictionary and thesaurus (recommended by Ruth Turman).
- *Blue Ocean Strategy: How to Create Uncontested Market Space and Make the Competition Irrelevant* by Kim W. Chan and Renee Mauborgne. Harvard Business School Press, Boston, MA (recommended by Betsy Blakney, Brent Hunt, David Sotolongo).
- *Collapse of Distinction: Stand out and move up while your competition fails* by Scott McKain (recommended by Betsy Blakney).
- *Crossing the Chasm, 3rd Edition: Marketing and Selling Disruptive Products to Mainstream Customers* by Geoffrey A. Moore (recommended by Sandy Pullinger).
- *Designing Powerful Training: The Sequential-Iterative Model (SIM)* by Michael Milano with Diane Ullius (recommended by Amy Barden).

- *The E-Myth: Why Most Small Businesses Don't Work and What to Do About It* by Michael Gerber (recommended by Mike Parkinson).
- *First, Break All the Rules: What the World's Greatest Managers Do Differently* by Marcus Buckingham and Curt Coffman. ("So many books attempt to provide formulas for success. This book looks at the differences in people and speaks to building on those differences rather than trying to fit everyone into one single, homogenized approach to leadership. It recognizes the importance of outcomes rather than prescribed steps for getting there. I recommend it to all my employee managers as a tool for developing their people" –recommended by Meg Dwyer). (Recommended by Tom Skrobacz).
- *Flawless Consulting: A Guide to Getting Your Expertise Used* by Peter Block (recommended by Amy Barden).
- *Freakonomics: A Rogue Economist Explores the Hidden Side of Everything* by Steven Levitt and Stephen Dubner (recommended by Kavita Khanna).

- *From Insight to Action: Six New Ways to Think, Lead, and Achieve* by Jean S. Frankel and Gabriel Eckert, CAE, ASAE: Association Management Press; 2012 (recommended by Betsy Blakney).
- *Funky Business Forever: How to enjoy capitalism* by Kjell Nordstrom & Jonas Ridderstrale (recommended by Sandy Pullinger).
- *Getting to Yes: Negotiating Agreement Without Giving In* by Roger Risher, William Ury, and Bruce Patton (recommended by Ruth Turman).
- *Good to Great: Why Some Companies Make the Leap…And Others Don't* by Jim Collins (recommended by Lisa Pafe, David Sotolongo, Mike Parkinson).
- *How to Become a Rainmaker: The Rules for Getting and Keeping Customers and Clients* by Jeffrey J. Fox (recommended by Chris Simmons).
- *How to Win Friends and Influence People* by Dale Carnegie (recommended by Jim Edwards, Mike Parkinson).

- *Jump Start Your Business Brain: The Scientific Way To Make More Money* by Doug Hall (recommended by Chris Simmons).
- *Kill the Company: End the Status Quo, Start an Innovation Revolution* by Lisa Bodell (recommended by David Sotolongo).
- *Kotler on Marketing: How to Create, Win, and Dominate Markets* by Philip Kotler (recommended by Mark Amtower).
- *Management* by Peter F. Drucker (recommended by Tom Skrobacz).
- *Never Eat Alone and Other Secrets to Success, One Relationship at a Time* by Keith Ferrazzi with Tahl Raz (recommended by Betsy Blakney).
- *Now, Discover Your Strengths* by Marcus Buckingham. ("I read this book when it first came out and have gone back to it many times. I really like that it encourages individual strengths rather than suggesting that a good leader (or individual contributor) needs to mold herself into a 'one size fits all' approach to be successful. I have used this to help differentiate myself

within my own work environment and to build extremely high performing teams." Recommended by Meg Dwyer).

- *Nudge: Improving Decisions About Health, Wealth, and Happiness* by Richard Thaler and Cass Sunstein. ("I highly recommend this book. It's written from a blended perspective of psychology and economics and talks about all the kinds of ways we are nudged into making certain choices. While they say it's a book about "Improving decisions about health, wealth, and happiness" it has some pretty obvious business applications!" Recommended by Julia Quigley).
- *On Writing Well, 30th Anniversary Edition: The Classic Guide to Writing Nonfiction* by William Zinsser (recommended by Amy Barden).
- *Powerful Proposals: How to Give Your Business the Winning Edge* by Terry R. Bacon and David G. Pugh (recommended by Chris Simmons).

- *Predictably Irrational, Revised and Expanded Edition: The Hidden Forces That Shape Our Decisions* by Dan Ariely (recommended by Mike Parkinson).
- *Presentation Zen: Simple Ideas on Presentation Design and Delivery* by Garr Reynolds (recommended by Chris Simmons, Beth Wingate).
- *Purple Cow, New Edition: Transform Your Business by Being Remarkable* by Seth Godin (recommended by Mike Parkinson).
- *Rain Making: Attract New Clients No Matter What Your Field* by Ford Harding (recommended by Colleen Jolly).
- *Resonate: Present Visual Stories that Transform Audiences* by Nancy Duarte (recommended by Chris Simmons, Beth Wingate).
- *Rich Dad Poor Dad: What The Rich Teach Their Kids About Money That the Poor and Middle Class Do Not!* by Robert Kiyosaki (recommended by Colleen Jolly).

- *Secrets of Power Problem Solving (Inside Secrets from a Master Negotiator)* by Roger Dawson, Career Press, 2011 (recommended by Betsy Blakney).
- *Selling to the Government: What It Takes to Compete and Win in the World's Largest Market* by Mark Amtower (recommended by Mark Amtower).
- *The Art of Possibility: Transforming Professional and Personal Life* by Rosamund Stone Zander and Benjamin Zander (recommended by Tom Skrobacz).
- *The Art of the Idea: And How It Can Change Your Life* by John Hunt (recommended by Ruth Turman).
- *The Daily Drucker: 366 Days of Insight and Motivation for Getting the Right Things Done* by Peter Drucker (recommended by Mark Amtower).
- *The Effective Executive* by Peter F. Drucker (recommended by Tom Skrobacz).
- *The Great Work: Our Way into the Future* by Thomas Berry (recommended by Tom Skrobacz).

- *The Happiness Advantage: The Seven Principles of Positive Psychology That Fuel Success and Performance at Work* by Shawn Achor (recommended by Colleen Jolly).
- *The Naked Presenter: Delivering Powerful Presentations With or Without Slides* by Garr Reynolds (recommended by Chris Simmons, Beth Wingate).
- *The New Rules of Marketing and PR: How to Use Social Media, Online Video, Mobile Applications, Blogs, News Releases, and Viral Marketing to Reach Buyers Directly* by David Meerman Scott (recommended by Mark Amtower).
- *The New Why Teams Don't Work: What Goes Wrong and How to Make It Right* by Harvey Robbins and Michael Finley (recommended by Lisa Pafe).
- *The Small-Business Guide to Government Contracts: How to Comply with the Key Rules and Regulations . . . and Avoid Terminated Agreements, Fines, or Worse* by Steven Koprince (recommended by Mark Amtower).

- *The Tipping Point: How Little Things Can Make a Big Difference* by Malcolm Gladwell (recommended by Mark Amtower, Mike Parkinson, Sandy Pullinger).
- *The Visible Expert* by Lee W. Frederiksen, Elizabeth Harr, and Sylvia S. Montgomery (recommended by Mark Amtower).
- *Think and Grow Rich: The Landmark Bestseller – Now Revised and Updated for the 21st Century* by Napoleon Hill (recommended by Jim Edwards, Mike Parkinson).
- *Think Out of the Box* by Mike Vance and Diane Deacon (recommended by Lisa Pafe).
- *Who Moved My Cheese?: An Amazing Way to Deal with Change in Your Work and in Your Life* by Spenser Johnson (recommended by Ruth Turman, Maryann Lesnick).

Enjoy these suggestions—many made my personal reading list (and kept me reading late into the night!).

Suggestions from readers – more favorite business books

Beth Wingate

After publishing my latest list of colleagues' recommended books, I received a number of additional suggestions from readers. Here they are for your business reading pleasure with links to Amazon.com so you can learn more and hopefully find some new favorites.

- ***Made to Stick: Why Some Ideas Survive and Others Die*** by Chip and Dan Heath (recommended by Jayme Sokolow).
- ***Start With Why: How Great Leaders Inspire Everyone to Take Action*** by Simon Sinek (recommended by David Stearman).
- ***The Challenger Sale: Taking Control of the Customer Conversation*** and ***The Challenger Customer: Selling to the Hidden Influencer Who Can Multiply Your Results*** by Matthew Dixon and Brent Adamson. (Both are well worth reading a couple times by

capture professionals pursuing large deals. Recommended by David Nealey).

- *Creativity, Inc.: Overcoming the Unseen Forces That Stand in the Way of True Inspiration* by Ed Catmull and Amy Wallace. (It talks to the successes and failures behind Pixar. It has some great lessons and advice on leadership and working with creative teams. Plus, if you like the movies (or have children who do, or both!) you get some great insight into their development. Recommended by Kevin Switaj).

Ready for some inspiration? 13 lists to find your next good book

Find your next business book or summer read

Beth Wingate

I'm never without a book in my hand—well maybe not while paddling my kayak—but that's about it! I vividly remember the day in 2nd grade when Mrs. Neman, the librarian at our local library, called my Mom to report me for trying to check out books that were "too precocious" for my age. I was flabbergasted that someone wanted to keep me from reading and learning about something new—I think it was a couple of books about spies or race car drivers or astronauts (all careers-of-choice to my 7-year-old self)! My Mom's response? "Let her check out any book she ever wants to read!" I've never looked back!

If you take a look at my e-readers (Kindle Voyage, iPad Pro), you'll find a plethora of business books on marketing, social media, design, knowledge management, program management, creativity, graphics, leadership, programming… If you look at my *fun* books, you'll find thrillers, adventures, steampunk, mysteries, histories, fantasies, cookbooks, travel guides, romances, dyeing, weaving, knitting, spinning…

What do they all have in common? They help me to expand my skills, broaden my horizons, think, ponder, grow, create, dream…

I'm always ready to try a new book. Here are some good book lists I've come across lately—I hope you'll find some new inspiration (and perhaps a great *vacation read*) among them!

- ***21 Books That'll Get You Ahead at Work, According to Top Career Coaches*** (https://goo.gl/R379ZZ) from Jody Powowski writing on The Muse website (Check out this website—lots of great content and a nice daily newsletter).
- ***15 Books for Creative Leaders*** (https://goo.gl/OQKlZm) by David Slocum writing on Forbes.com.
- ***12 Best Books Every Leader Needs to Read*** (https://goo.gl/E3dDbM) by Geoffrey James

writing on Inc.com (He also has a list of ***The 18 Best Motivational Books Everyone Should Read*** (https://goo.gl/kO3mLP) compiled from his readers' suggestions).

- ***NPR's Book Concierge – Our Guide to 2015's Great Reads*** (https://goo.gl/vtMaLn) produced by Nicole Cohen, Rose Friedman, Petra Mayer and Beth Novey (I like this list because I can hover over an image of each book's cover and get a *snippet* of the review and then click the link to the full book review).
- ***It's All Geek to Me*** (https://goo.gl/KzGJCP) from NPR.org (This is one of the filters available on the NPR favorite books lists to explore various titles. I've found some interesting books using this filter!).
- goodreads (https://goo.gl/JsAOli) has a collection of "***Best Book Lists***" (https://goo.gl/sqlKLl) voted on by goodreads readers that ranges from "Best Books Ever" to "Best Science Fiction of the 21st Century" to "Best Steampunk Books" to "The Most Influential Books in History" and everything in between. (Careful, though. You can get lost in the lists and

only resurface hours later! Allow plenty of time to explore the contents!)

Here's the list of recommended books I put together for my recent presentation H*ashtags, mentions, endorsements…oh my! How to use social media to build your personal and corporate brand* at APMP Bid & Proposal Con. Definitely check out Guy Kawasaki's book!

- *The Art of Social Media: Power Tips for Power Users* by Guy Kawasaki and Peg Fitzpatrick
- *Content Marketing – Think Like a Publisher* by Rebecca Lieb
- *Content Rules – How to Create Killer Blogs, Podcasts, Videos, ebooks, Webinars (and More) that Engage Customers and Ignite Your Business* by Ann Handley and C.C. Chapman
- *27 Facebook marketing mistakes businesses make and how to fix them* by Jim Edwards
- *The New Rules of Marketing and PR: How to Use Social Media, Online Video, Mobile Applications, Blogs, News Releases, and Viral Marketing to Reach Buyers Directly* by David Meerman Scott

- *The Social Customer: How Brands Can Use Social CRM to Acquire, Monetize, and Retain Fans, Friends, and Followers* by Adam Metz
- *Social Media for Business* by Martin Brossman and Anora McGaha
- *Social Marketing Superstars – Social Media Mystery to Mastery in 30 Days* by Cydney O'Sullivan

Finally, here are lists of favorite business books provided by my industry colleagues.

- From the experts: Favorite business books to start off 2016 (https://goo.gl/jVssHR)
- Suggestions from readers | More favorite business books to start off 2016 (https://goo.gl/Zxkgsf)
- Top 10 Favorite Business/Proposal Development-related Books (https://goo.gl/zXVKWq)
- Lohfeld Team's Favorite Business, Proposal, and Design Books (https://goo.gl/vAlDmF)
- More top proposal books for proposal writers (https://goo.gl/4J9hHt)

Q&A with Lohfeld Experts

Q&A from 7 secrets from inside government source evaluations and how you can use them to create winning proposals

Lohfeld Business Winning Webinar Q&A with Wendy Frieman

Do you know how the government really evaluates proposals? Have you ever wondered what they look for when they read through each offer and what they like and dislike when scoring proposals? Not knowing this makes submitting a proposal to the U.S. Government like firing a shot across their bow. What happens on the *other side* is a mystery to most contractors, and debriefs often don't tell the whole story. Or, even half the story! This is because those who prepare proposals and those who evaluate them have vastly different perspectives.

In this webinar, we released the results of our 3-year research project on how the government evaluates proposals and what capture and proposal managers need to know in order to create better, higher-scoring proposals and win more highly competitive bids. Watch the webinar replay to hear former Lohfeld Principal Consultant Wendy Frieman provide lessons from the *other side of the divide* based on 3 years' of interviews with acquisition personnel who have read and evaluated proposals with values up to and exceeding $1B. She explains 7 secrets learned from the other side and shows you how you can use these to up your competitive game. Below are the questions received during the webinar and answers from Wendy.

Watch the webinar replay and download the presentation and research brief (https://goo.gl/s7fLGW).

Q: How is information organized and presented in winning bids? Is there a magic formula? Is it all about compliance with the evaluation criteria as they are presented, or is it more important to tell a story for a more emotional buy-in?

A: I love this question! No, there is no magic formula. Winning bids come in all shapes and sizes, and any proposal manager who is honest will tell you that there are always surprises—proposals that seemed dead on arrival turn out to be winners, and vice versa. Stories keep the evaluators reading, which is a good thing. But, stories won't compensate for an absence of material that maps directly to the evaluation criteria. So, I would start with the foundation and then build the house. Address the evaluation criteria first. Then tell your story.

Q: *How does the government assess risk with regard to proposal responses? That is, how does the government determine the "riskiness" of a proposal?*
A: Good question. This was not the subject of any of my questions, but it came up repeatedly in answers. It appears that proposal teams regularly underestimate the degree to which source selection teams are risk averse. Of course, what constitutes a risk is highly subjective. But, if the perception is there, the fear will overwhelm the stated evaluation criteria.

Q: *Is there a standard to which the source selection board members must adhere, e.g., government contractors must adhere to the Federal Acquisition Regulations (FAR)?*

A: Yes, the people on the board have to follow the FAR. However, the FAR provides guidance that is open to interpretation.

Q: *We hear about automated evaluation tools—what tools are used, and when/how are they used?*
A: There are basically two categories of tools: 1) those used to help the non-price evaluators, and 2) the pricing tools. Both are used, and there are contracting officers who will discuss the use of the tools. It depends on the particular agency and office involved.

Q: *What is the evaluator expecting when the solicitation has 50 pages of "shalls" and you have a response limited to 30 pages?*
A: This is a great question, and one we all struggle with. There are many ways to address requirements. First, it depends on what kind of RFP you are responding to. Not all RFPs require or suggest that you write to every single "shall." That format is more common in product or commodity bids. If you do need to respond to every "shall," you can aggregate them in a table or refer to them by their RFP paragraph number to save space. If you don't have to address each individually, I always recommend sorting them in priority order and allocating your page count accordingly. This demonstrates knowledge of the

work because it shows you know what is important.

Q: *Who provides oversight to ensure the evaluators are really using the evaluation criteria provided in the RFP?*
A: The contracts shop has this responsibility. It is exercised differently in different organizations, but there should be training and well-articulated guidelines in advance of each source selection process.

Q: *How much subjectivity is there in what is supposed to be a very objective process? What's the latest "thing" in government procurement evaluations?*
A: There is subjectivity, but it is hard to say how much. The people I interviewed portrayed the process as fair, rational, and objective—perhaps because of a wishful-thinking bias. Although there are regulations, processes, and training, ultimately human beings are performing the evaluation and they are, well, human. This is why it is extremely important to find out as much as possible about who is participating in the source selection process.

My interviews did not focus on trends, but I think everyone in the business has noticed increased sensitivity to the potential of a protest. This drives a lot of the source selection process.

Q: *Can you discuss, from your perspective, why companies do not invest in formal capture management as a discreet function in the process of new business acquisition?*
A: Although this was not within the scope of my interviews, my impression is that it takes time to show the return on investment for a disciplined capture process. Many companies just don't have the staying power.

Q: *Is it your experience that evaluators are using electronic word search functions to evaluate proposals? Does this mean that we should avoid rephrasing concepts for readability in favor of parroting back the exact phraseology to meet the word search function?*
A: In general, it is best to use the terminology from the RFP to the extent possible. However, it is also important not to repeat the RFP requirements word for word, and many RFPs warn against this. So it's a balancing act.

Q: *I would love for you to address the situation when the government publishes an RFP riddled with so many errors and, during the Q&A window, refuses to cooperate and it is apparent that the contracting officer (CO) will not be making the needed clarifications by the*

consistent response of "bid as shown" or "refer to RFP." How many times and ways can you badger a response out of the CO without ticking them off?
A: Great question! If the RFP ambiguities have to do with contractual or pricing issues, I would stay on it and not worry about too much badgering. If you don't win, you will have a paper trail showing that you tried to clarify.

If the questions are about the non-price factors, I use a three-part test. First, is the question itself going to reveal anything to my competitors? If yes, don't go any further. Second, can I submit a compliant proposal without getting the answer to the question? If yes, stop there. Finally, can I live with the worst possible answer to the question? If so, then I would ask the question, but only once. As you have seen, often the answers that come back just make the RFP less clear. The best strategy is to state your understanding of the RFP clearly. That is a better use of time and energy than badgering a CO who probably cannot answer the questions in the first place. I think it is less about annoying the CO and more about how best to use the finite amount of time afforded for the RFP response.

Q: Is there a difference between the evaluation process used by DoD and Federal Government clients? Do

artistic cover pages make a difference since they are not part of the evaluation?
A: There are differences among evaluation processes even within the same agency and contracts shop. The FAR allows for this, and often the idiosyncrasies are not documented in any way that contractors can see. I did ask my interview subjects about proposal covers, and they all said that covers make no difference.

Q: *Our company has received evaluation notices regarding our sister-subsidiary connections for evaluation of both past performance and management approach. Understanding how best this can be presented to receive higher ratings and to avoid questions would be of interest to me.*
A: This was outside the scope of my interviews. Typically, the evaluation teams consider many sources when they are rating past performance. I suspect that it would depend on how close your organization is to its sister-subsidiary and how much they have in common with you. If you both do the same kind of work for the same customer, this could be a problem. In general, when there is bad past performance, the best way to deal with it is to show what you learned from it and how you improved your processes or technology to avoid a recurrence.

Q: *What do the evaluators really do with an executive summary?*
A: The executive summary can be a quick reminder of what is in the proposal and a roadmap that makes life easy for the evaluators. That is always a good thing. However, if it is not evaluated, it probably doesn't make sense to spend too much time on it.

Q: *I hear so much about the importance of a good executive summary. Do you have any specific recommendations for government responses?*
A: I dealt with this to some extent in the webinar. Typically, the executive summary is not evaluated. Evaluators find it helpful, however, so it might influence the way they see other factors. Also, it can be very helpful for the team because its creation forces a distillation and concise presentation of different concepts. It is not worth spending too much time on, however.

Q: *Does the government review executive summaries required by the RFP when there is an LPTA selection criteria (especially when the executive summary is not scored)?*
A: Executive summaries are rarely evaluated, but they can be helpful to the source selection team if the proposal is long or complicated.

Q: *We often hear that, "Evaluators don't read proposals, they score them," or that they don't have time to read, so they skim. Generally, we take this to mean that they look for compliance to requirements and responsiveness to specific criteria, strengths, risk reducers, key benefits, facts, and proofs—the things that allow them to make a fair and objective decision quickly. This all makes sense. However, our company, and most of the major capture/proposal consulting companies still offer training on writing for proposals that does touch on writing mechanics. Does good, clear, concise writing (active voice, direct, plain talk, short-to-medium length sentences/paragraphs, small words when appropriate, etc.) truly matter to evaluators?*
A: I did not ask this specific question. What I learned is that the evaluators appreciate anything that makes their job easier. As they are hunting for material that relates to the evaluation criteria, concise writing makes a big difference. It makes the proposal easier to score. So, I like your approach of active voice, short words, and plain talk very much. It is consistent with what my interview subjects said they appreciated.

Q: *Some folks in industry say storyboarding is dead. What are your thoughts on that, and if you don't use storyboards to bake in themes from the beginning, how do you write a winning proposal tailored for you client?*

A: Good question. I stopped using storyboards because instead of helping the writers, the tool took on a life of its own and became an obstacle. I like using an annotated outline based on the evaluation criteria. I have found that the best way to introduce themes and discriminators is to plan for many iterations. Start with a compliant proposal. Then add all the bells and whistles.

Q: *Do you think the fear of protests has elevated the amount of scrutiny on valuations/evaluation boards to make them more unbiased?*
A: In a word, yes. I did not ask this question specifically, but the importance of defending the scores assigned to each proposal came up many times in my discussions. Interview subjects cited instances when the team wanted to award a contract to a particular company because there were features they liked, but they couldn't find a way to assign points against the evaluation criteria.

Q: *I have always heard about word search software being used and how if you are too graphic intensive that the software can't pick it up. How pervasive is this?*
A: I did not ask about this specifically. But, to be safe, I would make sure that important compliance items are addressed in text as well to the extent that space permits.

Q: *How ubiquitous are checklists to evaluators as compared to more general subjective assessment of responses?*
A: Checklists are very common, but for compliance and not for evaluation against subjective criteria.

Q: *What would be the average level of specific knowledge of the services being procured by the typical evaluator?*
A: There are almost always some generalists on the evaluation team because the SMEs are very busy and often overcommitted.

Q: *How much training does the typical evaluator (general and specific) receive prior to performing his/her evaluation?*
A: The level of training varies widely, but there is always just-in-time training for the entire team.

Q: *How closely does the classical "color" team approach used in proposal preparation mirror the client's evaluation process?*
A: I believe that color teams in industry are quite different from the source selection evaluation team, for reasons I tried to explain in my webinar.

Q: *How consistently and closely do evaluation plans follow Sections L and M? When L and M track, is it safe(r) to assume the evaluation will be largely* *consistent with the instructions and criteria? Does the acquisition team prepare them, or the evaluation team, or a legal team? When are they prepared—with the RFP or when someone gets around to it AFTER the RFP is finalized?*

A: I believe I addressed some of these question in my webinar. Evaluation plans are part of the acquisition process and are prepared ahead of time. You can find general guidance on these in FAR Part 15 and in various entries in ACQuipedia (https://goo.gl/GtHRjy) at the Defense Acquisition University website.

Q: *What advice do you have when Section L and Section M are not aligned? Which should take priority in your proposal outline at the top level when they are in conflict.*

A: This question is debated endlessly by those of us in the field who go to proposal conferences and discuss proposal *theory/ideology*. I did not address it directly in my questionnaire. However, I try to organize according to Section M first. Then I address those items in L that are not also in M; but, if there are space and time constraints, I invest much more heavily in the Section M topics. Of course, some RFPs make it difficult to do this. It's a constant frustration.

Q: *How do your evaluators rate "desired/preferred" qualifications that the bidder's proposal might not meet?*
A: Good question. I am afraid I don't have a good answer. This did not come up in my interviews. However, I always treat "desired" or "preferred" as "required," because I figure that this is how my competitors will interpret that language.

Q: *In structuring the source evaluation teams is there general acquisition guidance that contracting officers use to help them decide the size or composition of those teams, or is it just who is available regardless of competency?*
A: There is very little in the FAR about how to structure the team. This is up to the contracting officer, and each agency and office has its own process.

Q: *How do you write a technical proposal that addresses each task in the Performance Work Statement (PWS), but avoids just reiterating the PWS, particularly with fairly non-technical requirements (for example administrative support services)?*
A: This is the art and science of good proposal writing! The answer is different every time, depending on the format of the proposal and the products or services being sold. For non-technical services, I would amplify what is in the PWS by

showing exactly how the work will be done, how it will be supervised, where your organization has done this successfully in the past and with what results.

Q: *If the evaluation criteria for past performance is neutral because you don't have any, would that be a reason to not bid (assuming that competitors had good past performance)?*
A: This was not covered in my interview questions, however, I would not bid in this scenario. It is true that you will be rated neutral, but other companies will have positive ratings, which puts you at a disadvantage.

Q: *Can you elaborate on protests of source evaluation board decisions—how to protest-proof your submittal?*
A: I did not ask this question. However, it appears that avoiding a protest is really the responsibility of the government, not the bidder. The best the bidder can do is to adhere closely to the proposal instructions and evaluation criteria (which presumably you would be doing anyway).

Q&A from The end of the incumbent empire – 10 ways to unseat the incumbent

Lohfeld Business Winning Webinar Q&A with Lisa Pafe

In the past several years, incumbents have lost their advantage in the Federal Government market. Industry studies show that incumbent contractors now have approximately the same win rate on rebids as non-incumbents. Rapid technological change, as well as fiscal constraints, mean that customers are more willing to consider alternatives. Still, winning a bid against an incumbent contractor is a challenge because the *best informed wins*, and the incumbent is still the best informed.

In this webinar, Lisa Pafe, CPP APMP Fellow and Lohfeld Consulting Group Vice President, provided 10 proven best practices to create a competitive edge over the incumbent in today's changing environment. Below are the questions we received during the webinar with answers from Lisa Pafe.

Watch the webinar replay and download the presentation and research brief (https://goo.gl/uXf7IU).

Q: *How do you approach clients that are not accessible and you are directed to only talk to the Small Business Liaison?*
A: Ask the Small Business Liaison to help set up meetings for you. Remember, each "customer" is comprised of business, contracts, technical, and budget stakeholders. Get your foot in the door with at least one of these, and always have a follow up action—such as a white paper.

Q: *Many contracts are simply getting extended by contracting officers. How do you prevent the extension to the incumbent?*
A: You cannot prevent an extension to the incumbent; however, an extension gives you more time to work on your capture.

Q: *Which of the 10 approaches are best for professional services in government contracting? Which of the 10 approaches are best under Lowest Price/Technically Acceptable (LPTA)? Which of the 10 approaches are best under Best Value (BV)?*

A: All of the 10 approaches work for professional services and for both LPTA and BV. The main difference in LPTA is that you must focus more attention on having the absolutely lowest price, thus requiring much more competitive analysis.

Q: *What is the current win rate for incumbents providing professional services?*
A: The research on current win rates does not break the data down by type of services. Assume incumbents win 30–50% of the time.

Q: *Are contracting officials required to disclose incumbent/follow-on order information such as Award IDs upon request? If so, is there a best practice on how to go about requesting this information?*
A: If the procurement is not classified, then award information is considered public. If the contracting official will not answer your questions, you can typically research incumbents using subscription services such as GovWin or Bloomberg. You can also try publicly available tools such as FedSpending.org or USAspending.gov.

Q: *Are there unique strategies that may apply when a small business competes against a large business incumbent on an unrestricted procurement?*
A: It is very difficult for a small business to compete with large business incumbents on an

unrestricted procurement. As a small business, you would need to have a truly unique value proposition that provides more strengths than the incumbent and no weaknesses. You could try teaming with partners that fill in gaps and/or providing lowest price, but unless you have pre-positioned yourself very well with the customer, in most cases it will be an uphill battle in overcoming perception of performance risk.

Q: Discuss typical information sources to obtain intelligence on incumbent performance and customer requirements. Do you have a list of recommended open sources for competitive intelligence information? What alternative intelligence gathering methods might you recommend when you are not able to get an audience with the programs people or contracting officer? For example, how can you find out about how the incumbent's current performance is perceived, business problems that are still not resolved by the current contractor, pricing information, etc.?
A: You can typically research basic information on incumbents and customers using subscription services such as GovWin or Bloomberg. You can also try publicly available tools such as FedSpending.org or USAspending.gov.

Other sources include:

- Incumbent web site
- Customer web site
- Job posting sites
- LinkedIn
- Facebook
- Twitter
- Press releases
- Annual reports/financial reports/investor information
- Conference publications
- White papers
- Industry news magazines
- Newspapers
- Talking to current and former employees and contractors.

Q: In a procurement for services, other than price, what differentiators can set you apart from the competition? In today's environment, what is the best way to make an impression on a government decision-maker prior to

the release of a procurement? What is the number one capture "must do" to put yourself in position to be successful on a bid?
A: You can differentiate yourself by proposing better and/or more strengths that benefit the customer by exceeding requirements, helping meet contract or mission requirements, and/or offering value-add. You make an impression by positioning your strengths with the customer during the capture phase. The best method to use in crafting your solution is focusing on building the greatest number of strengths and mitigating all weaknesses prior to RFP release. The number one "must do" is to position and shape your value proposition by listening to the customer.

Q: *Do you have a particular location in proposals that you recommend inserting a differentiation from the incumbent?*
A: Differentiation should be evident throughout the proposal. Every section should have win themes that include your differentiators with substantiation.

Q: *Is it best to always propose some percent of incumbent capture if it's optional (I know sometimes you HAVE to offer incumbents a position).*
A: I recommend stating that you will work with the customer to understand incumbent employee

skillsets versus those needed for the new procurement. You should propose to capture at least 90% of qualified incumbents. Back this up with evidence and examples of where you have achieved similar incumbent capture rates.

Q: *Do you have any advice for a small business that has recently graduated from the 8(a) program and must now learn to thrive and survive as "just another small business"? It is often said that to win in the government contracting game, a company must partner-partner-partner. With shrinking defense budgets, and all-too-common partnering, what should small businesses do to differentiate themselves into a competitive advantage?*
A: My best advice is to get on as many multiple award vehicles as possible so that you can compete with a smaller pool of pre-qualified vendors. Partnering is definitely important in order to fill capabilities gaps. For each opportunity, you need to assess honestly whether you can differentiate yourself with a value proposition that addresses customer hot buttons. If you cannot, perhaps take a step back and consider a market strategy assessment.

Q: *Do you think it is better to write an executive summary before the proposal is written or after the proposal is written? How can we better write to the*

client, especially in the executive summary? It is about them not us.
A: Many companies place too much emphasis on the executive summary, which is typically not evaluated. Instead, before writing, concentrate on identifying features, benefits, and proofs corresponding to customer hot buttons. Next, determine which the evaluator would score as strengths to ensure you have as many strengths as possible and no weaknesses prior to writing. Once you have identified this information, you can write a better executive summary and a better proposal.

Q: *Generally speaking, what is the pricing someone desiring to beat an incumbent has to get to (percentage wise) to be in the ballpark for unseating an incumbent? What does history tell us?*
A: The market is seeing incumbent price erosion of 15–30%. Therefore, your price to win should likely be at least 15% below what was bid on the original contract, adjusting for any revised levels of effort or scope.

Q: *Anything you can offer on the proper way to approach incumbent staff—as a group, individually—would be very helpful.*
A: As the challenger, you must be very careful not to disrupt the workday of the incumbent staff. The

best approach is to reach out to incumbents through LinkedIn. You can also hold group open houses after work near the office locations (advertise on your website and through LinkedIn messages).

Q: *How best to determine the incumbent weaknesses in the eyes of the client?*
A: Ask the customer (business, technical, contracts, budget stakeholders) what problems they are seeking to solve with the upcoming recompete procurement. What contract or mission objectives do they have? After RFP release, look for clues such as requesting new levels of effort, increased certifications and training, different scope, and the like. Try to reach out to teaming partners as well as current and former employees for additional insights.

Q: *How does a small business with limited past performance citations respond to RFPs that require three or more citations.*
A: The best approach is to team with a company that can provide additional past performance citations. If you cannot fill this capability gap, then make a no-bid decision.

Q: *How do you offset incumbent strengths with customers (the love fest)? How do you encourage competition with the government customer? What ideas and methods help craft your solution?*
A: The best way to offset incumbent strengths is to propose better and/or more strengths that benefit the customer by exceeding requirements, helping meet contract or mission requirements, and/or offering value-add. You encourage competition by positioning your strengths with the customer during the capture phase. The best method to use in crafting your solution is focusing on building the greatest number of strengths and mitigating all weaknesses prior to RFP release.

Q: *One of the hardest steps for large and small businesses who first encounter an opportunity at the RFP/RFQ stage is the bid/no-bid decision. The hardest thing about that—if you don't see the opportunity until the RFP/RFQ is published, which is late in the game—is deciding if the opportunity is wired or not. What are the top three ways to assign a probability of a given opportunity being wired and therefore not worth investing effort?*
A: If you do not know about an RFP/RFQ before it is issued, then you are at an extreme disadvantage regarding customer intimacy and competitive assessment. Therefore, your win probability is

below 10%. A rule of thumb is to no bid if you have no previous knowledge.

Q: *How can an incumbent best counter the tendency of a customer to be "too" fair by walling out the incumbent early—even after good performance—while giving competitors a chance for dialogue?*
A: Even if the customer *walls off* the incumbent, the incumbent can still do an honest assessment of its own performance. Tap into the knowledge of your program/project manager as to what is going on. The program/project manager and his/her team have daily access to a variety of stakeholders, giving them information that the challenger cannot easily access. Encourage the on-site team to engage in informal dialogue and report back to the capture manager.

Q: *How do you build customer intimacy when the incumbent already has a strong relationship with the customer—especially if they are on site and you can only access the customer by appointment or industry events? What about when the leadership declares they are happy with the incumbent and doesn't want to go through the huge pain of transition to another contractor especially when they are making progress? What about when the leadership declares they are happy with the incumbent, but when you talk to mid-level leadership they are not as thrilled and somehow their*

frustrations are not being clearly communicated up the ladder?
A: You cannot achieve the same level of customer intimacy as the incumbent. You must counter customer intimacy by building a strengths-based solution and ghosting incumbent weaknesses. Statements regarding happiness with the incumbent do not necessarily translate into a higher-scored proposal by the Source Selection Board. Focus your proposal on proving that your solution has the greatest number of strengths and no weaknesses with low performance risk.

Q: *How do we compete in the world of LPTA contracts?*
A: Part of your shaping effort during capture should focus on why the opportunity should be best value rather than LPTA. If the customer still insists on LPTA, focus more of your resources on Price to Win. If you cannot execute successfully at the lowest price, then do not bid that opportunity.

Q: *How does LPTA play into your strategies? How do you convince a client they get what they pay for? Many bids are going to the lowest bidder technically acceptable, and in many cases the clients are not satisfied with the work or products they get. We are finding too often that awards are being delivered based on cost, not necessarily best qualified. We understand*

from a business standpoint that delivering the best-qualified people, though it may cost a client a little more money, in the end can reduce the bottom line. How do you overcome this obstacle?
A: Part of your shaping effort during capture should focus on why the opportunity should be best value rather than LPTA. Convince the client by providing substantiated proof that the work cannot be performed successfully at lowest price. Make your business case and provide concrete examples.

Q: *How does the strength of the commercial economy affect this dynamic? If the commercial economy continues to strengthen, will it tend to reverse this trend?*
A: I would wager a guess that as the economy strengthens, the pendulum will switch back to best value procurements, thus favoring the incumbents.

Q: *How do you surpass the benefits that the incumbent has in terms of customer knowledge?*
A: The best way to offset incumbent strengths is to propose better and/or more strengths that benefit the customer by exceeding requirements, helping meet contract or mission requirements, and/or offering value-add. You encourage competition by positioning your strengths with the customer

during the capture phase. The best method to use in crafting your solution is focusing on building the greatest number of strengths and mitigating all weaknesses prior to RFP release.

Q: *I'm interested in how these best practices translate to the state/local market—also, how to turn the tables if we are the incumbent.*
A: The best practices discussed do translate to the state and local market. Within the next 2 months, I will deliver Part 2 of my webinar, which will focus on how to protect your position as incumbent. I will address your question at that time.

Q: *I am interested in strategies to overcome the knowledge gap, including ways to get the buying organization to level the playing field.*
A: The best way to overcome the knowledge gap is by conducting a listening campaign—meeting with a variety of customer stakeholders to suggest solutions, listening to their responses, and then shaping your solution accordingly. You can also gather information by researching and then connecting with current and former employees and contractors using LinkedIn, Web searches, and customer/incumbent websites. The customer will have incentive to level the playing field if they like the solutions you are offering during capture.

Q: *Is there a common mistake that incumbents are making that opens the door for them to be unseated? Are price cuts the main way that companies are taking incumbent business? What role do subcontractors play? Are they leaving the incumbent team and going to the competition? Do incumbents change the core subcontractors for recompetes?*
A: The biggest mistake the incumbent can make is to assume the customer loves them. Price cuts are certainly a large part of challengers' taking away incumbent business, along with proposing innovations that drive efficiencies. Subcontractors are leaving incumbent teams a bit more often now if they see a challenger offering a better value proposition (for them and the customer).

Q: *What usually drives the desire to change the incumbent contractor? What signs should a contractor look for as harbingers of likely changes with an incumbent?*
A: Perceived inefficiencies, high prices, lack of innovation, high staff turnover, lack of technical skillsets, and lack of responsiveness are among the many drivers of change. Harbingers of likely change include a customer that is very open to meeting with challengers, conducts extensive market research, and changes the work scope and/or level of effort.

Q: *What is the one thing that irritates evaluators the most about incumbents' proposals?*
A: The one thing that irritates evaluators most is to repeatedly state that you are the incumbent rather than proposing a thoughtful solution.

Q: *What are the questions you should NOT ask the customer? Said another way, are there dumb questions that can effectively knock you out of consideration, or that give away too much to your competition?*
A: Instead of asking the customer what you can do to help them, suggest solutions and listen to their reaction. Ask very specific questions that require them to answer with examples. By moving from general to specific questions, you generate a higher level of engagement and more thoughtful and detailed responses necessary to gain the insight you are hoping for from a customer.

Q: *What is the best way to gauge your percent chance of winning against an incumbent?*
A: Use a SWOT analysis to generate a better understanding of strengths and weaknesses versus the incumbent and other competitors. If strengths far outweigh weaknesses, and you have a plan to mitigate your weaknesses prior to RFP release, the win probability increases. Another method is to identify and then assess progress

towards key performance indicators for successful capture.

Q: *What is the best way to gain access to an incumbent client when they don't want to meet with anybody?*
A: The best way to gain access is by conducting a listening campaign—meeting with a variety of customer stakeholders (remember, there is more than one customer) to suggest solutions, listening to their responses, and then shaping your solution accordingly. You can also gather information by researching and then connecting with current and former employees and contractors using LinkedIn, Web searches, and customer/incumbent websites. The customer will have incentive to level the playing field if they like the solutions you are offering during capture.

Q: *When a government agency publishing a solicitation has a preferred vendor in mind prior to releasing the solicitation, what is the best means of capturing the proposal evaluators' attention so that they give my company's proposal an open-minded evaluation?*
A: You can differentiate yourself by proposing better and/or more strengths that benefit the customer by exceeding requirements, helping meet contract or mission requirements, and/or offering added value. You make an impression by positioning your strengths with the customer

during the capture phase. The best method to use in crafting your solution is focusing on building the greatest number of strengths and mitigating all weaknesses prior to RFP release. The number one *must do* is to position and shape your value proposition by listening to the customer. In an LPTA procurement, the biggest factor other than cost is past performance.

Q: *You mention that 50% of incumbents are losing in the federal world. Do you have a statistic about incumbents in the commercial world?*
A: No, unfortunately it is much harder to gather information about the commercial market because contract awards are not publicly available.

Ask the experts – your top business development, capture, and proposal management questions answered

Recently, Bob Lohfeld, CEO, Lohfeld Consulting Group and Bill Gormley, President and Managing Partner, The Gormley Group discussed various challenges faced by business development, capture, and proposal professionals supporting Federal Government contractors.

Read the Q&A, watch the webcast, or listen to the podcast to find out how to help your company work smarter and reinvent what you're doing to remain competitive in today's GovCon market.

Watch the webinar replay and listen to the podcast (https://goo.gl/AGWDSp)

Q&A – Initial comments

Bill Gormley: I'm honored to be here with you today and to be invited here on behalf of The Coalition for Government Procurement and The Gormley Group.

Bob Lohfeld: I'm particularly intrigued by the leadoff topic here—*Breaking into Government Markets*. If we talk about the market, it's a great topic to lead off with. I would conjecture that it's harder today to get into the government market than it has been historically, and it's harder for two principal reasons. One is the market is smaller today. It's been in a steady downhill slide if you're watching the federal budget numbers—the dollars that we can address as contractors. And the other reason is the market is moving ever persistently behind this closed umbrella of multiple award and GWAC contracts.

The good news if you're in the club and you have these vehicles or multiple vehicles, then your market is very flush with opportunity, and if you're one of the thousands of companies that doesn't have these kinds of vehicles, then it's difficult.

Bill: Then I think it's safe to say that you can't just walk in. So, in regards to that you have to have some kind of a business plan. No different from building a house—you have architectural plans. So for folks in industry that we've met with, Bob, over the years, it's still sort of amazing how people expect that they start their company up and think the government is going to come knocking on their door. It doesn't work that way. Ironically, you have to have a plan, and I think part of the plan is actually knowing what you're going to offer from a solution standpoint, and we'll talk about this a little later also. But when there is an opportunity to talk with a government official about what you're offering, don't make the mistake of just expecting that they're going to agree with you right away. You have to demonstrate an ability to offer a solution for them that lines up with their mission.

Bob: And you're absolutely right, Bill, because the market for companies that have good offerings is still good. It's still a $100 billion market in the IT space, and you can add professional services to it as well. It's a robust market.

Q&A Part 1: Breaking into government markets

Question: *How does a company get in to work with a new organization with the government so bound by bureaucracy?*

Bill: Well, I think first off there's that kind of mystique of government versus the private sector and practices. And to be quite honest, having been on both sides now, there are a lot of similarities. The larger a company, the more bureaucracy there's going to be. So the government is a big institution, there's no question about it. But, I think you need to break it down and start to understand where you align with what their mission is, and if you can demonstrate your solutions or services to what they're focusing on, the better you're going to be able to have that discussion with the government official.

Bob: I would add to it that this notion that companies should build a capability statement and then go around knocking on every door in government saying, "Here's what we do. What would you like to buy?" is really an offensive tactic—offensive and not welcomed at all by government. They want to hear you talk about issues, problems, and technologies of specific interest to them.

Bill: And I think—it's an obvious point that I'm going to make—but, I think sometimes it's important to bring it back to the forefront, it is taxpayer money. So with taxpayer money, there's going to be a level of oversight that typically is not involved in the private sector, and I think that somewhat maps to a longer sales cycle from industry in working with the federal government. So I think to keep that in mind—once you start having success, then you can play off your past performance. And for those listening who have had a lot of success from a past performance standpoint, you understand that you still don't go at the market in a shotgun approach. You want to be very strategic in how you go to the market because there is a lot of bureaucracy, but a lot of it is brought on by not understanding that specific agency's mission.

Bob: I'd say there are probably two steps here. First, you do the market research, figure out what the government's buying, what you want to sell, and why they should buy it from you. But, the second step is you have to have a way of closing the deal, and GSA Schedule is the premier vehicle for doing that for early entry into a government market.

Bill: In that regard, it's whether you're a startup or a long-term contractor or company. To Bob's point, the [GSA] Schedules is kind of your Better Housekeeping Seal of Approval where you meet all representations and certs required of the typical government contractor, so that begins the major step forward in you validating yourself in the federal market to any government contractor and any government user.

Question: *I would like to be provided some specific details on how to get meetings set up with the government. We are usually told networking, industry days, etc., but these are very generic and do not give specific examples on how we can actually get meetings set up.*

Bill: Well, there's still only one guarantee in life, but the fact that you want to get a meeting set up—you want to be sure you get meetings set up with the right people or right person. And when I use the term influencer, it's not to be taken in a wrong way or unethical way. It's someone who relates to what you offer, and whether there's an RFI out on the street or whatever the reason is that you have the interest in this agency, make sure that you get to an influencer. Anybody's going to be willing to talk to you to a point, but in order to understand what you're going to provide and what their needs are, the influencer is a key. The second part is once you're in, don't blow it! You're going to have that first impression. You've got to have an instant connection message when you meet with someone that validates who you are and your knowledge of that agency.

Bob: One of the government CIOs told me that she was really receptive to meetings with industry. She would meet with anyone who called and the protocol was 5 minutes into the company's presentation, someone would walk in the room and whisper in her ear, "5 minutes," and then she would look at them and say, "I'm so sorry. The administrator has just called me into a meeting and I have to leave." And out she would go. Make a good connection straight off!

Question: *How important is it to have a relationship in an agency before submitting a bid?*

Bob: Relationship is great if you have it, but it's beyond the relationship that's important. It's understanding what that customer wants to buy, why they want to buy it, what will make your offer a great fit for them, and what your competition is likely to do. It's that holistic package of deep, rich understanding that will trump the relationships. Our motto here is often quoted as, "Best informed wins." Having a good relationship helps you get informed, but the objective is *best informed wins*.

Bill: Yes. I think there are a lot of myths out there. But in this regard, if it's posted and I don't know about it or the requirement, then it's already set up with someone else and the probability of my winning it or participating is not high. I'm not going to say that people don't already know about it before it goes out on the street or help work on the requirements, but I guess the key is *relationship* from a professional standpoint—and name recognition, which will sometimes also qualify you. But really being able to demonstrate how you align with that official and that agency is a key part to establishing a relationship.

Question: *How can a company zero in on the right agencies and RFPs to focus on when getting started in the federal market?*

Bob: This is sort of like a comment somebody made to me once. They said they wanted to buy a house, and I asked them, "Where?" and they said, "North America." And I thought that's not very helpful from a shopping point of view. It's the same thing with government agencies. There are maybe 1,400 different buying organizations loosely connected under a set of federal buying rules, and each one is a little different with different needs and missions. A little bit of market research goes a long way into narrowing down that big ocean and giving you a chance to focus and identify people you need to connect with.

Bill: Yes. To follow on to Bob's point, pick your spots and how your service and solution will meet or exceed the agency requirements. In regards to the pricing side, I've had recent conversations with some folks in industry on certain government requirements where you have to have an approved financial system to do cost plus other than fixed fee. Do pay attention to the requirements by that agency out there, and see if you align with them and it's not a struggle to meet their needs. If it's pretty much in your swim lane, then you just dive in for it.

Bob: We have a whole set of criteria about helping you pick the right RFPs. Just because you see an RFP doesn't meet that it's right for you. There's a whole triage and qualification process that we take companies through to ensure that they're bidding deals that they can win. The best way to be successful is to pick the deals well that you're going to pursue.

Question: Do agencies pay attention to RFI responses?

Bill: Yes—the short answer. They are paying attention to it from an agency standpoint. From your point of view, you want to provide certain information—feedback—and it's nice to hopefully have a relationship (getting back to an earlier question) with that office and understand the intent of this RFI. Is it for a recompete? Are they looking at doing some market research before they exercise an option to make sure that they're still in line with the market? So, I think that's where your business intuitiveness comes in or kicks in from a business development standpoint. So, you want to be responsive. You want to see how the socioeconomic side fits in possibly to the size of your company. Obviously, get the best fit to win from your perspective.

Bob: A lot of people in government tell me they're disappointed in industry's response to RFIs, and when I see how a lot of companies respond, I can understand that. They take the RFI, bump it down to the junior person in the group, and say, "Write something and send it in."

Bill: Yes. I think this is not necessarily RFI—it's RFQ—but it somewhat gives further validation to what Bob just indicated. On RFQs—I think GSA's eBuy averages just less than three responses per RFQ, and that's a very, very competitive market. So to Bob's point, I think a lot of people look at it where they're not going to be eligible to compete when really the government is looking for more competition.

Bob: You have a great chance to shape the RFP, shape the evaluation criteria, show an agency what's really important in the market, and raise your probability of win if you do a good job on the RFI response or the RFQs. So take them seriously, and don't delegate them down to someone who is *available* and that's their only qualification to respond.

Q&A Part 2: Topics in the news

Question: *Talk about the new DoD procurement reform document. What are the key things that we need to know?*

Bill: So Bob, I think you did a recent digest of Claire Grady's April 26 memo/directive (https://goo.gl/AFgnyB) out there to DoD on source selection.

Bob: I did, and that sort of narrows down the topic a bit. So the topic is DoD procurement reform, and reform is something we see at about a 10-year cycle across DoD. Every 10 years going back 40 years, someone is screaming, "We need to reform DoD procurement. Throw out the FAR and start all over." And these play through like a bad summer squall and then dissipate back to where people realize that the FAR is really good. What Claire Grady did (who works for Frank Kendall in Acquisition Technology and Logistics and basically is responsible for DoD policy) is restate a lot of their doctrine in source selection and add to it. One of the new things that we're seeing in DoD source selection is Value Adjusted Total Evaluation Price (VATEP). In a best value sense, instead of leaving it to the bidder's discretion to figure out how you exceed a requirement in a contract, what they're doing is telling you if you can exceed it, it's worth a certain credit to you in the price evaluation and they're monetizing the benefits now. We're seeing that come out in procurements where the requirements are easily measurable—like speed of a vehicle or less-measurable survivability in the defense sense. But where they can measure that performance requirement, if you can exceed it, they will tell you that's worth so many millions of dollars and it lets you as a bidder do a tradeoff. Do you want to exceed it or do you just want to meet the objective level?

Bill: I think in regard to that and your earlier point about the FAR, when people can stand aside and actually look at the FAR and read it (it's not something you want to read every day possibly), there's a lot of opportunity for judgement and decision making by the contracting officers. I think in some cases the government, while having good intentions to provide examples of how to conduct procurements, I think things have gotten overprescribed and hopefully Claire's April memo starts to stress the need for judgement in the contracting area. We indicated earlier that taxpayer dollars are associated there, so there's oversight and sometimes from an oversight perspective you can't do enough to have a rigid procurement so there's absolutely a level playing ground. So it's a balance, a continuous process here.

Bob: The comment about the FAR—don't read it like it's a novel. Read it in short segments. I was probably 20 years into business before I opened up the FAR and just started reading it, and it explained a lot of what I heard as urban legend, and it debunked a lot of what I had been told. It was a new day after reading the FAR and understanding what the government's doing. And it's shorter than the rules of golf, so have at it!

Question: *What is the future of LPTA—lowest price technically acceptable?*

Bill: I think in Bob's digest of Claire's memo, it talked about Frank Kendall and his *Better Buying* initiatives over the past couple of years when—and again this is where it becomes overprescribed—there was a mention of LPTA in Better Buying and it just took off like a prairie fire of, "Now we have to do LPTA." But, I think even Congress has gotten wind and has chimed in with, "Let's pull back from the emphasis on LPTA and try to get a balance back on best value and keep best value in procurements." Because at the end of the day, it's actually in the FAR—pricing is fair and reasonable. That's the bottom line—if the contracting officer can reach that conclusion and have all the technical requirements aligned with what the requirements are, it's pricing is fair and reasonable. So the LPTA pendulum has swayed way too far, and it's actually heading back to kind of where it should be. There's going to be a place for LPTA in some procurements—identical items or something like that—but people would still argue that even for identical products there are different delivery times and other measurements that could also play into making a final decision for award.

Bob: The great thing about Claire Grady's memo is that it really defines the criteria and really restates the criteria from the earlier DoD directive as to when LPTA is appropriate. In the services market, it's generally not appropriate unless it's some level of commodity services. What we're seeing now in the market, the last vestige of LPTA on a major procurement, was DISA's Encore and before the procurement closed and proposals were submitted, they received two protests, and I was delighted to see them. They challenged the evaluation criteria and said, "This is just inappropriate." You can see the pendulum swinging now, and it's swinging substantially because some of the legislation working through for the 2017 Defense Authorization Act is proposing that contracts be awarded without price at the vehicle level and leave price to be a shootout at the task order—that having pricing done at a large GWAC or multiple award contract level is really irrelevant.

Bill: And that really ties in the commercial practices. Where do we go anywhere and say, "How much are you going to charge me for X?" They're going to say, "Well, how much are you going to buy?" So you can't just go ahead and try to get the best deal without coming up with some kind of requirement to align with it.

Question: *Do you think the self-evaluation methodology used by GSA OASIS and Alliant 2 is the wave of the future for Government Acquisition Strategy to avoid bid protests like NETCENTS, etc.? What are the potential negative features of self-evaluation methodology and impacts on industry (small, mid, and large businesses)?*

Bob: I'm opposed to the self-evaluation methodology because to me the government sets up an attributes model and says, "Here's what we're looking for in terms of a company—all these different credentials" and then you measure yourself against that standard, which is to me like driving a car looking in the rearview mirror. It's all about what you've done in the past and not one thing about what you can do in the future—your innovation, your creativity, your insight, your knowledge, your new technology. All of this is left behind in this criteria. And it closes out all of the upcoming, upstart companies. It closes out companies that are envisioning creativity and leading their market and leaves it to those who have a long pedigree—an insiders club. The old guard club stands very well in the self-evaluation and the others don't.

Bill: So I guess what I hear you saying, Bob, is that when the government sets up a potential template and you just fill and check all the boxes and say, "I have the experience. I can self-certify" without really getting behind who a company is and what they have to offer, so there are other qualities and other attributes in there regarding the technical side.

Bob: For sure there is, and I always like the idea of evaluating companies on their technical approach, their management approach, and how they're going to do the work—not about their pedigree and about what they've done in years gone by.

Question: *What's your outlook for category management, which has been identified by the House Small Business Committee as having a negative impact on the small business federal contracting community?*

Bill: Category management is a commercial practice. I think we can all agree to that, but not on this scale. And so, understanding the administration is interested in the categories that they've broken out, they have a head for each category now, and that's part of the objective of where OFPP or the administration wants to take category management I think is understood. I think how to get there is yet to be determined.

There are a lot of trees that need to be removed to get some kind of a trail here because one of the problems is that the government in moving forward on category management doesn't have *spend* data. And it's not just spend data at an umbrella level, it's really getting down to the spend data by product and specific labor categories and the fact that they don't have the historical data in trying to do category management I think has been a challenge so far.

Bob: I think category management has good and bad in it. The good is that I think it's great for government agencies and different agencies to get together and compare notes about how they procure and lessons learned—that makes everybody stronger. When it devolves into this strategy of "Let's use existing contracts and push all our business to those," then it shuts out a huge segment of the market. In the long run, it's the old boys club prevails and everybody else can go home.

Bill: So I guess the innovation side is the concern because I know there were configurations for laptops and so forth, and there was a lot of discussion about that.

Bob: And the laptop argument was, "There are three contracts in place. You can choose any of the three, and across the three there are hundreds of companies that are contract holders." So if you're one of the fortunate ones you can play, and if you're not, then you go and ask to be a subcontractor somewhere else and hope you get a piece. But you can never grow up and be a prime.

Q&A Part 3: Small/mid-tier competition considerations—and what it means to be a large organization with contracts moving back into small business set asides

Question: *With the way that procurements are coming out now, what do you do as a mid-tier company? How do you compete or should you? Should you go small again?*

Bill: The NAICS codes are really size dependent, so you'll see you're either *small* or you're *other than small*. So *mid-tier* is a self-anointed term that in government regulations has no meaning. So, you're either small or you're large. So I think the key here is when you get into this graduation mode of going from small to large, there are a lot of unknowns. You should understand that in services, it's dollar-driven on products if you're offering that or people count-driven in terms of determining the size, and everyone should basically understand that. You should start planning your graduation from small to other when you start your company. If you don't have an end game when you start something, you never know where you are in the game and how long it's going to take. Sometimes we get lost in that and then what happens is, in meeting with many companies, they say, "Hey! We can no longer compete on set-asides!" I understand that. So why is that a surprise? "Well, we're mid-tier now." You may classify yourself as mid-tier, but the government doesn't recognize you as mid-tier. So no one's going to feel sorry for you.

Bob: That's true—and it's not a phenomenon in today's procurement market. This mid-tier issue's been around for 40 years, and every small business that graduates thinks they should get another helping hand here as a mid-tier contractor and often aren't ready to compete against the largest. The ones that are successful as mid-tiers recognize that graduation is coming, and as Bill says, they plan for it. They prepare for it. They begin looking to have procurements and contract awards that aren't set-asides in their business. They sharpen their pricing skills, and they sharpen their skills to write highly competitive proposals. And if they don't, then there's two trajectories left. One is that someone buys you if they can find some value in what you have created, or like many that reach this mark, they go out of business and just sort of gradually vanish, and you'll see them 2 or 3 years down the road with a third of their revenue and then it goes to zero and they're gone.

Bill: So it kind of boils down to having a strategic business plan from the beginning.

Bob: And for those who compete in the full-and-open, it is a tough, tough market played by the best and brightest athletes in this industry. If you're playing ball at the high school level, when you step up to play in the Big 10, it's a whole different game and you need somebody to see that, to visualize it, to internalize it, and to lay down a plan and execute the plan to say, "We have to be ready."

Question: *As a small business, how would a company get to the full-and-open competition when there is no size standard for mid-tiers?*

Bill: You have to start day one to go for full-and-open (and even if you're small, to gain experience and have success lessons). I know that business development and resources are limited, so you're not going to use a shotgun approach, but you should put your toe in the water and go after some full-and-open along the way just to get the lessons learned. Could be a negative lesson—a negative lesson later on could be used as a positive experience.

Bob: Stay focused in your market. Know what you do and do really well. Build a deep core competency in your company, and when you do that, then you can take on the larger players. When you look at deals—they come in different dollar denominations—pick one that's below the threshold of what becomes a key deal for a large company. So maybe $15 million is a good threshold number. In the large businesses, if the deals fall below $15 million, they're bidding them with a pickup team. They're bidding them with a project team and not applying those great corporate resources—the A players don't get into those deals—so your A Team can take them away all day long.

Bill: Part of it is also to make sure you get a debrief—even if you're a winner. If you don't win, you want to get a debrief so you start to acquire some lessons here.

Question: *What is the role of IDIQs for companies transitioning from small to large business?*

Bob: I'd say it's a must have in my view and it goes by market. If you look at the IT Services market, 60% of that market today is flowing through vehicles—the multiple awards and GWACs. In professional services, 40% is flowing through. So if you want to be in the swim lane, you have to have a vehicle to stake a claim.

Bill: Yes. I'd say that they play a key role in climbing, however you want to categorize it, or growing up in the business size corporate ladder. In other words, you have to play there in order to grow and to win. So it's *not to be ignored*.

Bob: And the new vehicles, as you watch the history of these vehicles, the period of performance keeps creeping out. In the early days, they were 3 years or maybe 5 years, and now they're 10 years with absolute acknowledgement that on the last day of your 10th year, you can book a task order that's good for 5 years.

Bill: In regards to your size, depending on where you are with a particular IDIQ, even if you can't fully deliver 100% of the requirement (I know it's hard and everyone wants to go in as a prime, that's understood), sometimes being a sub also gets you in the door and you can have adjacent services and become familiar with the customers as well. Don't forget that when you're a sub, the prime is always going to be looking at you.

Question: *As you transition projects from being a large business prime and may have to become a sub to a small business, how do you transition from prime to sub?*

Bill: You don't burn your small business bridges. There's been a lot of talk over the years of people bringing subs in and making them part of a proposal. They won the business, and they don't use their partners. This could come back on you if you haven't played fair in the market and at some point you need to become a sub. Don't burn those bridges.

Bob: As the primes that were small and have outgrown the size standard can't compete again, the work is going to go to a small business. You have one chance to pick a partner and collaborate and get half a loaf rather than what you had before. It's tough.

Bill: In regard to that, utilize your qualified small network partners. So to Bob's point, a network becomes very, very critical here and it gets back to what we talked about in the very beginning when we talked about relationships. It's not only relationships in government, but your relationships in the market.

Q&A Part 4: Capture/proposal processes

Question: *What are your suggestions for transitioning a company "set in their old ways of doing business" to a smarter and more competitive process?*

Bob: This is a great question because we see a lot of these processes that have atrophied within companies that were *good enough* in the good days. But as the market contracts, the competitive standards are increasing, and if companies aren't adapting their processes to the new competitive market, they're falling behind and will lose business. The market is indeed more competitive and we're stressing with companies they need to have a defined, repeatable capture process in place that they manage to and measure their progress along the way, and that becomes a great predictor of success down the road. Then we need to change this mentality in companies that what they have to do to win is write a proposal. What they have to do to win is write a very *high-scoring* proposal. That's a whole different game from just writing a proposal.

Bill: They have to be more focused in the market.

Bob: Sure they do.

Bill: So if your win rate goes down, what does that mean? You've got one or two things.

Bob: First it means you probably picked poorly the deals that you want to bid. That's the number one challenge when win rate drops or capture rate drops. Second is that you're writing proposals, you're pushing out a lot, and none of them is very competitive.

Bill: So if your win rate drops, is that more on the business development side or on the prep side of the proposal from your viewpoint?

Bob: Well this is where it's hard. It's on the executive side in my view. Your company leadership never saw an RFP they didn't want to chase, and as long as they're not working nights and weekends and you are, they'll keep the process going. That's where you've got to push back and say, "We only have so much human effort we can put in this. So we need to pick well. And if we pick well, we'll have a winning season." It's not like baseball where you have to play every game in the calendar. With proposals you pick the ones you want to play. You don't have to play every game.

Question: *Under what circumstances, if any, should a company respond to an RFP when it's had limited to no impact on the creation of the RFP?*

Bill: You know you can get into a fire drill here. You can run around, but—to use some of Bob's knowledge he shared today—you need to be strategic. You need to be smart about it and not chase everything. That's a danger there. But, I think if you haven't had any involvement, if it's a pretty straightforward opportunity and you're not really having to stress internally to go after it—maybe you've already provided similar solutions—I think it makes it an easier choice to go for it.

Bob: I would agree. Having an impact on the RFP is only one of 10 criteria that we look at. The others that are more important are how deeply do you understand the requirements and the needs of the agency, and how well does your solution match up. Those will trump whether or not you had an impact on the RFP.

Bill: So with zero capture, how does that affect commission on a salesperson?

Bob: Zero capture—this is really neat. If you explain to them that you want to bid this and you haven't done any capture but the top five competitors have been working this for a year and here's what they've done. Now do you want to jump in the race? Can you beat them in the last 30 days? I don't know. Maybe. I wouldn't bet my money on it generally, but that's what you're up against.

Question: *Can you share a streamlined bid/no-bid process that is effective for a 10-person business development team supporting a 200-person group?*

Bill: I know this is your sweet spot, Bob, but can I say something?

Bob: Sure!

Bill: I think you really need to maximize shared services models. There's a lot out there. So I think to not overstress the company from a resource standpoint, all companies use outside resources and it makes them more targeted in better leveraging resources internally. It may give you a greater opportunity for capture. That's my layman's experience on this, but you're the pro here.

Bob: We have a model that we use, and we recommend companies adapt their practice using our model as a starting point. You have unique capabilities in your company—your own specialized market—and you can improve the model. Our model is not a quantitative model. We don't believe that you get five points for this and two for that, and you add them all up and you have a score of 71 and you should bid. It is very much a model where the measures are qualitative. It's how well do you really understand the customer requirements. How well does the customer know you and trust you—that you can perform? It's these kinds of questions. We color score them red, yellow, blue, green and we use this color mosaic for making decisions. But a strong green or blue on understanding the customer's requirements trumps everything else. So in the end, the executive needs to make an informed decision.

Question: *How can you effectively incorporate lessons learned into your proposal development process?*

Bill: I'd say 100% of the time get a debrief whether you win or *not win*.

Bob: I always argue that you either win or you gain experience—there's no losing here—you're gaining experience.

Bill: You don't play; you don't get an opportunity to win.

Bob: It's an opportunity to learn.

Bill: Also document what in your debrief worked and why it didn't.

Bob: Here's the crazy thing. You get a debrief. The government explains to you where your strengths were and your weaknesses, and you share that with three of your closest friends, and that's the end of it. When we talk with companies about lessons learned, I tell them that what we're going to talk about are lessons *relearned* because you learned it before. It just didn't stick. You need to have a process where it's shared and the whole organization that competes for business understands what those challenges were and the problems and you come away with a game plan to say, "Let's not relearn this lesson next time."

Bill: I think a key takeaway on debriefs is do not get into an argument.

Bob: Yes. It's not a time to threaten to protest. It's a time to learn, and in all the debriefs I've participated in, I always tell them we're not here to protest. We are here to learn, so please help us. We want to do better for you next time. Try to set that as a tone to the meeting.

Question: *What are the value of "win-themes" in today's market? My company executives are highly engaged in the "win-themes" process, but I have seen some data indicating that this might be a task in which we are over-engaged.*

Bob: We did a study with people in government who evaluate proposals. We interviewed 40 of them under the ground rules that we wouldn't disclose the procurements that were involved or in any way have comments come back to them. The first question we asked was, "What do you think of our win themes?" To a perfect score—100% said, "What's a win theme?" So we came away from that with a different notion of what constitutes a great proposal, and we have to the best of our ability taken the term *win theme* out of our lexicon. What we talk about is *strengths* in the bid—features that can be scored as strengths—and we focus on those. Companies that are still dwelling and spending time on win themes, if they are other than strengths (which are conveyed as a feature, a benefit to the government that meets a narrow set of requirements, and a proof), then you're spending lots of time on the wrong things.

Bill: Interesting. So in that regard, you want to use your strengths side. I guess a win theme is elaborating on how good you are? Is that it?

Bob: Yes. It's a subtle story we've woven through our whole proposal to give you the feeling that we're *thought leaders*.

Bill: So you feel good about yourself when they've written this down. I guess.

Bob: Yes. Most authors do.

Bill: So then you use *strengths*. I kind of view it as *blocking and tackling*. You have to address what the government's looking for and that takes *strengths*.

Bob: This comes back to our concept of creating high-scoring proposals. You write a proposal to put points on the board, and companies lose sight of that. They write a proposal because in the RFP instructions, it says "write this." So we wrote it, and we wrote it really well. But, nowhere in there is any evidence that can put points on the scoreboard. So, we've long ago moved away from win themes, and we talk in terms of a compelling proposal that's rich in features that could put points on the board.

Q&A Part 5: General questions – business development, capture, and proposals

Question: What is your outlook on the market and the upcoming election?

Bill: On the election standpoint, regardless of who wins party-wise, from a government contractor budget impact, it's pretty much going to be negligible. There's not going to be any change. And the reason I'm saying that is because the budget for next year is already being worked right now. So whoever steps into the White House and takes over control of the government from a leadership standpoint, they have a budget that they're going to have to stay with through 2017. It's really going to be 12, maybe 18 months, before you really see any swing if there is going to be a swing. It would be by exception that you would see any drastic changes from a government-addressable market standpoint.

Bob: Let me put a little fine-tuning to that. In my experience, we're coming up on the end of an 8-year term of a president, so no matter what happens going forward, many of the political appointees in government agencies will be changed out. The leadership in government agencies—the *politicals*—realize that they have between now and the first of October to implement changes that they want to make, or maybe between now and the first of December. I often see at the end of an 8-year stretch renewed emphasis on buying and obligating money—and then that's the influx of transactions. We get a slowdown come the new election, the new president, the new appointments of *politicals,* and we hit a trough in the spending. So I think it's a little bit of an up wave and a little bit of a down wave on top of the 2017 budget.

Bill: I think this is not going to be a surprise to anyone, there's a high probability of a continuing resolution (CR). What the CR equates to from an addressable market standpoint is the government is going to buy at the level next year that it was buying at this year, which is October 1. Whatever it takes to run the government—that's always going to be out there and being acquired—so that's not going to go away. It's anything new, and getting to your point, Bob, if someone in a particular agency or a senior official says, "Hey! I'm going to get this program off the ground," you may see an RFP out or an RFI on it trying to get it launched beforehand. You can look for those, but I think those are going to be few and far between.

Bob: How many shopping days left in the year for the government?

Bill: Never enough!

Question: *With the shift in government procurement regarding category management, LPTA, and IT consolidation, traditional price-to-win approaches can prove inadequate. How do firms adapt their pricing strategies to compensate, remain competitive, and profitable?*

Bill: Well we're rolling up here a lot of what we talked about today, so we're not going to be any miracle workers in one sit-down session. A lot of it's going to be recognizing the way the government market is going. To Bob's several points he's raised, you need to be in step with it. You need to understand it. And, don't continue to fall back on past practices. So, it depends on how you're buying and how you're handling your HR resources internally or how you're managing your company—it has to change. But, that should not be news to anybody.

Bob: I think you have to know your customer as they differ in terms of their sensitivity to price. Some agencies will tell you, "We want best value. We want technical superiority." Then they turn around and award to the lowest price from the offerors time and time again. You have to separate the talk from the walk. That will help you set strategy. At the vehicle level, be fair and reasonable about it—about pricing—because the price evaluation is not so sensitive at a vehicle level, but the shootout is at the task order, and you have to know your customer and know what you need to do.

Question: *What is the main focus of capture and how do you start the process?*

Bob: Capture has two purposes. One is to get you ready to write the best proposal that you could possibly write. You start that out by getting together the smart people in your company, forming a capture team, and then getting deeply involved understanding this customer and this requirement. If you understand it better than anyone else, you'll create a better solution than anyone else. So that's where capture begins. The other part of it is to get the government prepared to award to you. I've always had this belief that we don't do business with people we don't know—or at least we try not to—and I think people in government share that. So during capture you have a chance to make yourself visible and make yourself credible as a player. Raise the expectation within government that you're going to provide this service or product that they want.

Bill: Basically, you're aligning to capture to align your internal resources and then also to be able to convey that to the government as to how well prepared you are to meet their requirements.

Bob: And if you do that overall, you raise your win probability. If you don't do capture, well, your probability of win wasn't raised.

Bill: Yes. The day of walking in and brand name recognition—I'm not saying it still doesn't have credibility today based on past performance—but I think other folks who are coming in with, from their viewpoint, more agile offerings are getting more attention today.

Bob: Yes. I would agree.

Question: *What is the ideal win rate percentage? Too high, not bidding enough or stretching—or too low, bidding the wrong or too many RFPs?*

Bill: This is a great question. There's no answer to it, number one. So let's start with that. But number two, the reason that there's no answer to it is in talking to some companies, I'll ask them what their win rate is. They'll say, "80%" and I'll respond, "80%! I'm surprised you aren't just building in the whole square block downtown! But let me understand something. How did you get the 80%?" And they'll answer, "Bill, it's a little secret. We're very, very selective on what we go for."

Bob: I wrote a paper on this in *Washington Technology* (https://goo.gl/wmW5tD) where the same question was posed, and I said if you're winning 80%, then you're not bidding enough. Open the aperture on what you're going to bid because you will be better off by bidding more, dropping your win rate, but you'll increase your revenue and you'll increase your return on investment. If you're down in the 20%, you're in the mud, and you've got some things that are really wrong in your business and probably without looking at your business, you're not doing a good job qualifying deals and you're chasing stuff you shouldn't chase. Second reason will be you're pretending to execute capture and you're not doing it. Instead of capture, you're tracking. Third reason is you're writing mediocre proposals one after another. All of those can be diagnosed and corrected within companies. We see a lot of companies run along at 50% or 60%, and I'd say that's really at a sweet spot. They're writing well, they're picking deals, and they're delivering value to their shareholders.

Question: *How do you introduce innovation to your customer when you're currently performing for them and you're coming up for recompete?*

Bill: On the innovation side, there's a lot out there where the government wants to be innovative, wants to attract innovation, wants to be agile—you hear all these words more and more. I think a key here—and it's a balancing act—is that the sight to go agile does not align with oversight, because the oversight folks are not agile and they get a little nervous. They're looking at structure on the oversight and that's from a procurement standpoint. They have people who are always looking over them seeing how well they're doing. So, to get to the question, how do you offer up [innovation] and be considered, I think it really boils down now to the relationship you have with that customer and in a nice way conveying how you're being restricted from being more agile and making that customer better. So that's a dicey area, but it should be pursued because the government is out there saying, "We want to tap into Silicon Valley. We want to be more agile." And obviously we're seen recent things in the press about where people have tried to be agile getting criticism, so some of that's going to go on. So I think if you have a contact in the agency who's willing to listen to you and consider it and give you the opportunity, then you should actually pursue that.

Bob: One of the steps in capture is testing your solution with the customer to the extent you can. Here we want to validate our assumptions and test the water with some innovative ideas. I've had customers say to us when we've done this, "Well, we like two of the three ideas. The third one—we tried that before and we'll never go there again." That's the kind of insight you need to know. Your innovation can be very scary to a customer that's not ready to have you come in and change how they do business. So, test it. Be cautious about it. But work hard to come up with it.

Watch the webinar replay and listen to the podcast (MP3) (https://goo.gl/qu79tR)

Listen to the podcast on your tablet/phone (MP3) (https://goo.gl/asyDLi)

During the webinar, Bob referenced a number of articles to assist government contractors:

- 7 questions to answer when making bid/no-bid decisions (improve your win rates) (https://goo.gl/9B5YPk)
- Win rates double with seven quality measures – updated (Lohfeld seven quality measures) (https://goo.gl/JZ2AH2)
- DoD revamps source selection process (https://goo.gl/ujB6N4)
- DoD releases new Source Selection Procedures (https://goo.gl/3NCxvH)

Our experts:

Bob Lohfeld, CEO and Founder, Lohfeld Consulting Group

Bob Lohfeld serves as CEO and general manager of Lohfeld Consulting Group. He has more than 30 years' experience winning contracts in the government market and is recognized consistently for leadership in business development, capture management, and winning proposals development. He teaches Capture Management, and he writes the *Capture Management* column in *Washington Technology* (https://goo.gl/9A2OwX).

Prior to forming Lohfeld Consulting Group, Bob served as Division President at Lockheed Martin, Vice President of Lockheed Martin Information Technology, Senior Vice President at OAO Corp., Systems Engineering Manager at Computer Sciences Corp. (CSC), and Program Manager at Fairchild Industries. He also taught at the graduate level at George Washington University School of Engineering Administration.

Bob has served on the Board of Directors for the Association of Proposal Management Professionals (APMP) and Association of Proposal Management Professional National Capital Area Chapter (APMP-NCA), as Chairman of the American Council on Technology Industry Advisory Council (ACT/IAC), Vice Chairman of the Technology Council of Maryland (TCM), and Board Member of the Armed Forces Communications and Electronics Association (AFCEA), Government Electronics and Information Association (GEIA), and Juvenile Diabetes Research Foundation (JDRF Capital Region). He is a three-time winner of *Federal Computer Week's* Federal 100.

Bill Gormley, President and Managing Partner, The Gormley Group

Bill Gormley is a 40-year veteran of government procurement. He spent 28 years at the GSA in positions ranging from procurement agent to Senior Executive (SES) Assistant Commissioner for the Office of Acquisition. He was responsible for acquisition policy and all contracting operations, which included the Federal Supply Schedules Program. Bill's extensive experience re-engineering the GSA Multiple Award Schedules Program earned him recognition by both government and industry. While serving as Assistant Commissioner for the Office of Acquisition at GSA, Bill received both the Presidential Rank Award for Meritorious Executives and the Vice President's "Hammer Award" for changes to the Federal Supply Schedules Program. He was twice named to the *Federal Computer Week* Federal 100 awards—a prestigious group nominated by their peers for outstanding contributions to industry and government.

Bill left GSA to become President of the Washington Management Group (WMG). Shortly after joining WMG he purchased FedSources, a leading market intelligence firm for federal spending, and spent the next 11 years running both companies as President and CEO until both were acquired in 2011 by Deltek, Inc.

In addition to Bill's role as President and Managing Partner of The Gormley Group, Bill serves as Chairman of The Coalition for Government Procurement and Vice Chair of the Procurement Roundtable. He is a lifetime member of the National Institute for Government Purchasing (NIGP). Bill has contributed to the publication of two books related to the GSA Schedules Program and is recognized for his GSA Schedules domain expertise.

Acronym Glossary

Acronym	Definition
APMP	Association of Proposal Management Professionals
B&P	bid and proposals
BD	business development
CMMI	Capture Maturity Model Integration
CO	contracting officer
CONOPS	concept of operations
COR	contracting officer's representative
CO	contracting officer
COTS	commercial-off-the-shelf
CPARS	Contractor Performance Assessment Reporting System
CPI	continuous process improvement
D&B	Dunn & Bradstreet
DCAA	Defense Contract Audit Agency

Acronym	Definition
DOD	Department of Defense
DOL	Department of Labor
DOT	Department of Transportation
DTP	desktop publishing
FAR	Federal Acquisition Regulations
FTE	full time employees
G&A	general and administrative
HR	human resources
IDIQ	indefinite delivery, indefinite quantity
IR&D	independent research and development
ISO	International Organization for Standardization
IT	information technology
ITIL	Information Technology Infrastructure Library
JPL	Jet Propulsion Lab
LPTA	lowest price technically acceptable

Acronym	Definition
MS	Microsoft
NASA	National Aeronautics and Space Administration
NCA	National Capital Area
NDA	nondisclosure agreement
OCFO	Office of the Chief Financial Officer
ODC	other direct costs
OFPP	Office of Federal Procurement Policy
PDCA	plan, do, check, act
PMBOK	Project Management Body of Knowledge
PMI	Project Management Institute
POC	point of contact
PPIRS	Past Performance Information Retrieval System
PTW	price-to-win
QA	quality assurance
QC	quality control

Acronym	Definition
R&D	research and development
RFP	request for proposal
SaaS	software as a service
SB	small business
SF1449	Solicitation/Contract/Order for Commercial Items
SME	subject matter expert
SOP	standard operating procedure
SSB	source selection board
TA	teaming agreement
WBS	work breakdown structure